Finding Grace: The Journey to Self-Discovery

Riverhouse Books
St. Louis MO 63146
ISBN: 1-893892-03-4

© 2010 Cris Robins

All rights reserved. No part of this book may be reproduced in any form or by any means, electronic or mechanical, including photocopying, recording, or by any information storage and retrieval system, without permission in writing from the publisher or the author. This work is currently available in print and electronic form.

DEDICATION

It needs to be said first, that without G-d and His patience and His wonderful sense of humor, this work would have just been one of the many thoughts swimming around in my head that never went anywhere. This is my gift to Him.

I'm dedicating this book secondly to Laura Christian; not only is she a wonderful friend, she is an editor extraordinaire. In addition, where would I be without my best girl friend, Sue Clark? I'd probably still be stuck in the mud of my life. To her, a heart felt dedication as well. Then there is also one of my dearest friends, Kathryn Asbury who put up with the late night calls, the sobs over dinner, and the constant bombardments of "What did I do wrong, this time?" I couldn't be where I am without her help and support.

I'd also like to dedicate this work to my family, mainly for putting up with me through the trials and tribulations that they've helped me face.

Oddly enough, I'd also like to dedicate this to all the people who walked in and out of my life; for without them and the lessons they had to teach me, I'd have had nothing to write about and would not be the person I've become. It is my hope that those who read this work will find their own journey to becoming who they are; will know they are not alone, and will realize when you hit rock bottom, the only direction to go, really is up.

A NOTE FROM THE AUTHOR

Dear Reader,

I didn't set out to write this book; that was not my goal. What I set out to do was to relieve the pain in my life. I did that; one day at a time, sometimes one moment at a time.

And so it was, every day I would sit and write—not so much journal, but write—write about what was going on in my life, how I was feeling, what I was learning, and what I had to do to get me from where I was to where I wanted to be. Sometimes what I had to do was work through the past pains; other times it was to take advantage of new opportunities; and still other times, all I had to do was …nothing. I think that was the hardest thing of all.

My editor tells me I need to write an introduction; a set of reasons of why I wrote this work, what I hope to accomplish with this work, and what you, the reader, can hope to glean from this work.

I think she's right; I do need to do all of those things. So, I'll make it simple.

I was in pain; this relived my pain; it is my hope that if you are suffering that you may ease your pain in reading my journey; and most of all, that maybe, just maybe you can learn from my mistakes and not have to work through them as I did to Finding Grace.

Grace means a lot of things to a lot of different people; for me it is an acronym that changes with the month of the year; changes with the situations I'm dealing with; and changes as needed to give me focus.

It is my hope that you, too, will be able to find the grace you need to live the wonderful life you deserve.

With grace,
Cris

INTRODUCTION

This book will follow a calendar year, divided into 12 sections. Each section will re-define the acronym for GRACE. The book will actually begin in October. However, the cycle can be started in any month.

October	Time Out!	**April**	Growth
November	Gratitude	**May**	Courage
December	Miracles	**June**	Joy
January	Planning	**July**	Excellence
February	Acceptance	**August**	Fierce
March	Action/Adventure	**September**	Faith/Re-evaluation

At the end of each section will be the following 10 questions:
As you focused on GRACE this month, did you see a parallel to an issue in your own life? The following ten questions may help you gain new perspective on how to manage it.

Questions to ponder:
Is this issue bigger than me?
What is my part in resolving the issue?
Is now the right time?
What's stopping me?
How do I remove the barriers?
What resources will I need to get started?
What resources do I have?

Answers to Act on:
What isn't working?
What is working?
What's the next step?
To do List:

The purpose of this monthly summary is to help you assess any issue that may be bothering you. You are encouraged to use the blank space provided to find your own path to GRACE.

TABLE OF CONTENTS

Dedication 04
A Note from the Author 05
Introduction..06
Table of Contents..07
October 11
  TIME OUT!..12
    Self-pity is easy ... resilience is the tough part...13
    It's raining leaves..14
    The winter of my life.......................................17
    Grief-o-Meter..19
    Hope vs Faith 23
    Summary..25
November 27
  GRATTITUDE..27
    Listening to the Almighty 28
    Lifestyle 30
    The Extra Mile..33
    Giving Back..36
    The search for IT...38
    Summary..40
December..43
  MIRACLES..43
    Holiday Miracles...44
    Through the Eyes of a Child 47
    Closing the Book..50
    New Habits...52
    Visible changes 55
    Summary..57
January 59
  PLANNING..59
    Spring Planting...60
    Imposters 63
    Cycles 66
    Comfortable Shoes...71
    Productive or Busy? 74
    Summary..75
February..77
  ACCEPTANCE..77
    Rebuilding, again..78

  Good Broken 81
  Liberation 83
  Alone 86
  Play Time 88
  Summary 91
March 93
 ACTION/ADVENTURE 93
  Ten dollars worth of Motivation 94
  Decisions 96
  Mulligan's 99
  Confusion 101
  A Time to Do 103
  Summary 106
April 109
 GROWTH 109
  The Spoiled Child 110
  A Good Cry 112
  Teachers 114
  Dressed for success 116
  Miss Alice 117
  Summary 120
May 123
 COURAGE 123
  The Silence 124
  Wishful thinking 126
  Abandonment 128
  Fear 131
  G-d's Timing 133
  Summary 135
June 137
 JOY 137
  Worthy 138
  Rest 141
  New Dreams 145
  Stumblings 147
  A matter of class? 149
  Summary 151
July 153
 EXCELLENCE 153
  Accidental Lesson 154
  Quiet 156
  Better 159

Contentment	162
Solace	164
Summary	165
August	**167**
FIERCE (Fabulous & Fearless)	167
Pink is a state of mind	168
Kennel Club	172
The Little Things	176
Identity	178
Centered	180
Summary	182
September	**185**
FAITH AND RE-EVALUATION	185
Limits	186
Don't	189
Set in stone	191
Faith	193
The Struggle to NOT struggle	197
Summary	201
Closing Notes	203

October

TIME OUT!

October is a month of taking the time to pause and examine your life—decide what you do or don't like. During this time of assessment, focus on …

G   for GUIDANCE
R   for REGROUP
A   for ATTITUDE
C   for CANDOR
E   for EXPECTATIONS

SELF-PITY IS EASY ... RESILIENCE IS THE TOUGH PART

Wallowing in self-pity is easy.

Ask me; I know, because I did it for one hundred days straight, as well as on and off for the better part of the last year.

We find ourselves a reason – oh, my husband left me; my girlfriend dumped me; my boss fired me; I didn't get the promotion; I'm too poor; I'm too stupid; I'm too fat; I'm too thin; I'm too – you get my drift – and we use our reason, we milk our reason for all it's worth, as an excuse not to DO.

I'm not discounting your reason, not by any stretch, as I had my own; it was a perfectly justifiable reason for me to whine, and complain, and make my friends crazy, and drive potential friends away, and look to someone else for my own self-worth. But, it was only and simply – a reason to fail – one more reason why we didn't DO anything but fail; and because we failed we just confirmed our REASON for our failure ... then the cycle begins again.

We are so busy wallowing in our own self-pity, pining over a lost opportunity, that we turn to total strangers to validate our existence, and when even THAT doesn't work, we fall deeper into our pit of despair; we hit rock bottom. But—what if we took two minutes out of our self-pity and said: SO WHAT?

Would this be so horrible? Would addressing our reason with a "so what" be more painful than what we are doing now? Would looking at ourselves in the mirror and screaming, "MY HUSBAND LEFT ME – SO WHAT?" be so utterly earth-shattering our world would crumble in pieces around us? Would realizing nothing we do is going to change this fact be so horrific that we would turn into social jellyfish?

Or would it mean, quite simply, that now we have to DO something? We have to realize no matter what we do, we can never recover the lost opportunity. We have to pick up the pieces of our lives and move on. We are no longer stuck in our reason-groove, and we have to get past whatever it was that held us back and go forward. We are no longer afforded our REASON as a safety net for not doing.

October

So now that we know our REASON is no longer going to sustain or support our failure, what do we do? Once we have accepted this REASON as a fact, realized nothing is going to change this fact, and are looking at DOING instead of complaining, where do we go from here?

We face each challenge with our "So what" attitude. This doesn't mean we don't CARE about the outcome of whatever we are trying to do; it just means we realize when facing this challenge that if we fail, we will not be devastated by it to the point where we stop.

In sales there is a cute little ditty used to motivate the salesperson to pick up the phone. It's a mindset that says: "Some Will, Some Won't, So What? Someone's waiting!" In each of our endeavors, some will go our way, some won't go our way, so what if it doesn't, and someone is waiting … waiting for us to get to the point in our life where we need to be.

The first three SW's are self-explanatory; the last takes some thought. "Someone's waiting!" Hmmm. Someone is waiting for us to overcome this obstacle, whether it is to get over a husband's or a girlfriend's leaving, get a new job, a different position, get thinner or fatter, become smarter, get our finances in order. Whatever it is, someone is waiting for us to DO something.

Who is waiting? Is it a new husband, a girlfriend, a new employer, someone at a weight clinic, or at an educational institution, or maybe at the bank? Maybe it's someone from whom we can learn something, or a lesson someone needs to learn from us? Maybe it's someone we meet along our journey that may just be the best thing ever to happen to us? Or, maybe, just maybe … it's we, ourselves. That's right, us!

Maybe this obstacle is in our way to make us stronger, more self-reliant, more compassionate, more … something; and we're not becoming that something because we'd rather wallow in self-pity, pine over lost opportunities, and consume ourselves with analysis of what we might change to regain said opportunity. Or, maybe our obstacle wasn't what we thought it was, what we wanted it to be, but just what we invested in and lost. So what? This might be the most exciting time in our life because we are being given the opportunity to make a change, do something different, to become what only we can become, and now is the time to DO something to make it all happen.

After all, you don't know who's waiting for you.

Time Out!
R - Regroup

IT'S RAINING LEAVES

It's raining leaves.
Sort of.

From where I sit working out of my studio office, I can look down on the parking lot below me. The cool thing is the way the buildings are set up, my apartment is in the corner of one building and I can look across to the corner apartment in the next building. Well, between us are the garage doors, the dumpster and a few extra parking spaces; further out are a grassy area and a sidewalk, further out still is the adjacent office building parking lot.

But, today, what lies between us are leaves; lots and lots of leaves. I watch them swirl around in whirlwind fashion on the parking lot going from one building to the next and then completing the cycle again and again. Until ... a very strong gust of wind comes along and shoots them straight up into the air – higher, higher, until they are out of my sight (which would be about five stories up) and then they come down. They swirl lazily against the blue October sky, the bright fall sunlight glinting off their fire colors as they seek the shelter of the familiar – the parking lot floor.

Now most of them make it back down to start the same old cycle as they left – but, some, yes some don't. They go to one patio or the next – they end up in the grassy area – or the dumpster area – and some, yes, some even go into the next lot where the office building lies to start another adventure.

As I am wallowing in the problems of my own life, I start to wonder; what if each one of those leaves represented one of the problems in my life? What if like a big strong gust of wind I could blow them up and out of sight? Could I be like the big-bad wolf and huff and puff and blow them away? If I did, would some of them come back and seek the shelter of the familiar – would some go to the next patio – and would some, yes, some even go high up into the air and land on the lot next door never to been seen again?

What would I do with the ones that came back? Better yet, what if I could CHOOSE which ones came back and which ones went somewhere else? What if I were the wind? What if all of those problems were under my control and I could chose?

October

I didn't know – but – I did begin to huff, and puff, and I blew with all of my might, and imagined my problems shooting up into the air. As they came down I examined each of them and told them if I wanted them back – if I wanted them to go to another patio – and if I wanted them to go to the building next door.

The first to return to the familiar was the monthly bills – yeah, got to have rent, cars, utilities, and food. They were welcomed.

Then my education – of course! This was my pride and joy, my future we were talking about here. Certainly my education was welcomed back.

Next to the familiar was my business. Hmmm – this was a tough one. Yes, it was my job to solve the business problems – but, what if I changed the business? What if to make it to the familiar it now had to be something I enjoyed? Well, this would make a difference, now wouldn't it? This one I put on the patio and told it that it could come back on the condition it became something I felt good about; or would have to go away if it couldn't.

But then, there were my children. Hmmm. They were grown – one son had a family of his own. Was it still my responsibility to solve the problems of my children? No, they were adults – this is true; but, how close should they be? Or maybe, how far away should they be?

How close is close enough – yet – how far is far enough away? Is the patio too close or the office building parking lot too far away? As I looked at the parking lot, I saw this nice grassy area. Yes, that would be close enough to help, yet, far enough away to be separate.

Down the problems fell, and then came the hard ones. What about friends or other family members? Could I let those who were good for me come in and those that weren't go to the lot across the way to start their own adventure? What about my ex-husband and all the ex-boyfriends after him? Could I let go of all the toxic relationships in my life?

As I watched the next gusts of wind blow the leaves high up to the rooftop, I realized, yes, yes, I believe I could. And if I did, could it not be a good thing for all of us?

It was at that moment I realized – my problems really were under my control and I could decide which ones I would let come back to the familiar and which ones I wouldn't. I realized I'm not the Almighty – and as such – it isn't really my responsibility to solve everyone else's problems – just my own. I can choose which one of

Time Out!

someone else's problems I take on; and just as importantly how to give them back to them.

    I smiled. No, nothing really went away; but my load did get lighter when I chose only the problems that were mine, that I could solve, and realized that all the rest were just like so many leaves in the wind. ☺

A - Attitude

THE WINTER OF MY LIFE

It's winter now.
And it has nothing to do with month of the year.
Like winter, I feel dormant; as if I've stopped living my life, as if all that lay about me are the leaves of fall; my fall from grace as it were. I don't know what to do with the leaves; I don't know what to do at all.

I looked up the definition of winter and didn't like what I saw. It made me very nervous, especially the definition which read, "A period like winter, as the last or final period of life; a period of decline, decay, inertia, dreariness, or adversity." (www.dictionary.com)

Then I started to look at the reality of *winter*: a time to get away (to *winter* in Florida); a time of rest and rejuvenation (to hibernate for the *winter*); and to come in from the harshness of the world (as in plants who *winter* indoors).

I've always been one to note on rainy, dreary, cold days, that it's a great day for working as it's a lousy day to do anything else.

And maybe that is what winter is all about—a time to step back from the normalcy of our lives, to rest a bit more and clear our minds, to come in from the harshness of the world and rejuvenate our selves—our souls.

Maybe this is a time afforded us each year to evaluate where we are, where we want to be, and to slow down just enough so the universe can do its work.

The fall brought me the opportunity to shed a good many things in my life—personal relationships, old standards of behavior between me and my children; and some old grief's as well.

In this winter I look about me and am grateful for all that I've done, see some work yet to do, and feel that ever so slowly I'm putting the pieces together of the puzzle that will be my life.

I find I worry less, am not as afraid as I was, live more by faith than I have and realize that I really am okay.

So there it is. All about me is gray – skies, trees, grass – my life. Ahhh, but the hope is if I relax, do what is needed to be done,

Time Out!
take my time and do it right, then the spring will be an explosion of color, of life, of new beginnings. What more can I ask for?

C - Candor

October

GRIEF-O-METER

It's cold in my flat this morning.

So, as I got another cup of coffee and a fresh pack of cigarettes, I checked the thermometer. Sure enough, it was 67 degrees.

As I flipped the switch to the "heat" setting and heard the furnace kick in, I wondered: what is the thermometer for my life?

I'm pretty good when it comes to judging the temperature in my flat; if it's too cold, I check the thermometer and turn on the heat; if it's too warm, I check the thermometer and turn on the air-conditioning.

So, what do I check and before making adjustments when it comes to other issues in my life? In business, I called it my grief-o-meter. When a staff member, client, or vendor caused me more grief than they did joy they were gone. But, did I ever really use it? I know it was there, like some thermometer in the background, quietly doing its job. Did anyone ever trip my grief-o-meter so grossly that I fired them?

Once. At the time my staff numbered eight, and we were all housed in one room of a relatively small office. It was an open office space with high ceilings, Casablanca ceiling fans, and a wall of windows; I didn't put people in cubicles. I liked my staff. Not only did they do a very good job for me, but there was also a comfortable level of friendship amongst us. I remember sitting at another's desk in the back of the office helping them with something and noticing the new woman was sitting not far from me filling out all the paperwork one completes when they first start a new job.

I was grateful she was here as there was one task that needed to be completed before noon, and no one else had the time to do it. It was a very simple task. A 450-page manuscript needed to be three-hole punched and placed in a three-ring binder. It wasn't rocket science, but, it still needed to be done.

The din of the office was a comfort to me; it meant everyone was working and doing what they do best, concentrating on the task at hand. Without warning, her voice was heard above all. She turned

Time Out!

to the Business Manager and asked, "Do you want to see my driver's license?"

He was confused, and asked, "Why?"

Without skipping a beat, she said, "To prove I'm not a (explicit for illegal alien)."

You could have heard a pin drop in that room. The silence was tangible. Slowly, I turned my chair to face her. "What did you say?" I asked in a slow, measured, tone.

She repeated herself and started to explain to me what it meant.

"I know what it means," I said, "I just can't believe you said it."

She continued to justify her remarks to the silence in the room.

Without realizing it, she had committed a carnal sin in my office; she had done the one thing I held tightly to a zero tolerance level; she had used a racial slur. As our firm was international and we often worked without the benefit of actually seeing our clients, I had made it a standing policy that racial remarks were not tolerated, period. The silence which engulfed the room was two-fold—the shock of the term coming out of her mouth and the expectations of what I was going to do about it.

Without another word I turned back to my task at hand, but, I was faking it. The thoughts were racing through my mind; I had to have her assigned task completed by noon; I couldn't tolerate her actions. Loud enough for all to hear, I said, "It's time to get back to work." The din ensued, but it was lower than normal.

I waited for her to finish her paperwork, and then took it upon myself to give her the manuscript to process. It took her until noon to do it. The office was still too quiet as the staff filed past my desk to leave for lunch; no one would look at me. As the Business Manager was leaving, I told him to get me the checkbook. He tossed it on my desk and left.

I stopped the new woman and did the only thing I could do; I paid her for her time, fired her, and told her never to cross my path again. There was no other choice. My staff returned from lunch and gave a collective sigh of relief when they saw she was gone.

When they seated themselves back at their desks, I stood in the middle of the room and addressed them. "I will NOT tolerate racial remarks!" I paused. "It is beneath all of us."

The Business Manager quietly said, "You know we couldn't figure out why you didn't fire her on the spot."

October

"We needed her to do a job, and when that job was finished, we didn't need her any longer. It was a tough decision I had to make."

"We were going to quit," he continued, "if she was here when we got back."

"I would expect nothing less of any of you." The crisis was averted in that their boss lived up to her word; she made the tough decisions as they were needed; and didn't back down. All was right with their world.

Nothing less. What was the nothing less that now I expect of myself? I expect nothing less of me than to make a good living, to do work I enjoy, to provide services which make a difference, to pay my bills relatively on time, to associate with people who won't embarrass me regardless of whom we met, and to dress and act in such a fashion that all those who see me think highly of me.

How do I put that on a meter? Where is the gauge which judges the success of those issues? When have those standards fallen below or risen above "nothing less?"

If I look at the little things in my life it's easy to see where the meter is. When I go out in public, I dress for the occasion, whether that be oxford and blue jeans or a suit or somewhere in between. When I look about me at my flat, I ask, "Is this suitable for company?" The only acceptable answer is, yes. Does it make me uncomfortable when I look at the sight of my car as it's not as tidy or organized or with enough gas in it as I would like? Do I like having only but $20 in the bank at any given time?

It seems to me that the meter I use to judge "nothing less" is my comfort level at those items in those situations. I can excuse wearing my loafers outside of the house, if I'm just going to the mailbox. I can accept the trash not having been taken out, the laundry not being done, nor the floors attended to as I've been busy with final exams and projects; but that is a call to action to take the time to get those issues in order. Yes I can excuse a messy car if I've just gotten back from a trip to see my kids; but, it doesn't stay that way long. I can even justify only having $20 in the bank, if I've the $20 in my stash, the $10 in the change jar, and the bills caught up.

So, why don't I have a meter for the other issues in my life? Is it because I've not taken the time to make up a list of what I consider "nothing less." Am I failing to focus my attention in that area and so

Time Out!

am unsure of what falls short of "nothing less"? Or have I just been so eager and willing and accepting of others and grateful for that which I have received, even though I know they fall far short of my acceptable "nothing less," I accept it all anyway and just "make do?"

I've had enough of "making do" and settling for far less than "nothing less." I just need to know what adjustments to make. It's time I make the tough decisions, stood up for what I know is right, and make the plans to get back to where I belong.

I've been cold far too long.

E - Expectations

October

HOPE VS FAITH

"Dear G-d, please hear me."

"Hello, G-d. Thank you for all the good stuff you've given me, and the bad stuff that I'm learning from."

I realize, contrary to some popular structured religions, there is no right way to pray. However, I couldn't have been more stunned when I'd asked a dear friend of mine how he prayed, and he answered with the first example above.

The shocking thought that went through my head was, "As if He WOULDN'T?" It was beyond my realm of comprehension to believe that I could pray, and G-d wouldn't hear me. It bothered me for days that my method of prayer would be one of thanks, when another was asking, dare I say, begging, just to be heard.

I felt his opening sounded as if he were saying, "Please, G-d, if you've nothing better to do, and you've got a few minutes, and I'm so very unworthy, would you please consider, for just a moment, my menial life?" It was as if he was hoping that the Almighty would give him a moment of His time, and in the same breath doubting that He would.

I don't normally pray in any traditional sense of the word; actually, I've been accused of "talking" not "praying." Maybe it's because there is never any doubt in my mind that G-d hears me, understands me, and is there to help me find the way He has designed for me. The only problem is, I don't always understand what He wants me to do, so I'm in need of guidance when the road is rough or the decisions, many. I have faith that He hears me, and when I ask for help, He gives it to me.

Perhaps in this matter, the differences lay in that my friend hopes while I have faith; he wonders, and I have no doubt; he questions, and I obey.

Yet, I can't help but wonder, aren't hope and faith two-way streets? Not so much between hope *and* faith; but between humans and the Almighty? If we HOPE the Almighty hears our prayers, does He HOPE we will listen when He gives us direction? If we have FAITH what we are asking for will be resolved, does He have FAITH

Time Out!

we will do as He asks of us? If we KNOW He is there to help us, does He KNOW we will take His help when offered?

What if we stopped hoping and started to have faith? What if we had the courage to believe that not only does G-d hear us, but also has faith in us? What if we stopped hoping G-d will answer our prayers, but had the faith that He's waiting for us to ask for help? What if we stopped asking Him to hear us and just believed that He did?

What if there was no doubt?

Regardless of our religious beliefs, we all have a few things we can count on: G-d loves us, wants only the best for us, and has faith in us. Could we do no less than return the favor?

G-d does not have doubt in us; how can we have doubt in Him? Or do we just have doubt in *ourselves*? Why is it we can't believe G-d does love us, is available to us, and He has faith in us? Is it because we feel so very small, so very fragile, so very ... unworthy ... that we can't believe He can see the value in us, that He would have time for us, that He doesn't rejoice in helping us?

So why is it, we have the arrogance to doubt the ultimate Father? Why arrogance? Because how arrogant could we be to believe that we know what the Almighty believes more than He does? Why is it so very difficult for us to believe that even when we don't believe in us, He does?

Whether we want to admit it or not, we have to accept that G-d loves us as no one else is capable. We are his children. As our Father, maybe it is He who hopes we will listen, until such time as He can have faith that we will.

When we hope, we leave open the possibility of doubt; when we have faith, there is no doubt. Perhaps it isn't just a matter of having faith in the Almighty but needing to live a life so He can have faith in us. When we stop hoping and start having faith, we build the two-way street with the Almighty.

October

SUMMARY

As you focused on GRACE this month, did you see a parallel to an issue in your own life? The following ten questions may help you gain new perspective on how to manage it.

Questions to ponder:

1. Is this issue bigger than me?

2. What is my part in resolving the issue?

3. Is now the right time?

4. What's stopping me?

5. How do I remove the barriers?

6. What resources will I need to get started?

7. What resources do I have?

Time Out!
Answers to Act on:

8. What isn't working?

9. What is working?

10. What's the next step?

To do List:

November

GRATTITUDE

November is a month of being grateful—of recognizing all the good things in your life, even the ones that are not immediately obvious or obviously good. During this time of thankfulness, focus on …

- **G** for GRATITUDE
- **R** for REVERENCE
- **A** for AMENDS
- **C** for CHARITY
- **E** for EXCITEMENT

Gratitude

G – Gratitude

LISTENING TO THE ALMIGHTY

"I thought you were too screwed up to love anyone.
I was wrong. You just can't love me."

The words escaped my mouth and echoed in my head before I even had time to think about them. I hung up the phone and didn't answer it when it rang again as I knew it would.

I was tired; more than tired of trying to convince others I was worthy of them, that I was good for them, and hearing of all the reasons why they couldn't love me.

I was tired of the e-mails, the text messages, the late night phone calls which normally started off with them telling me how wonderful I was, which escalated to the various reasons of why I wasn't for them, and ended with them asking if they could come over.

Why in the world would I want to invite someone over who made it very clear they couldn't/wouldn't/didn't love me? Was I so lonely for human companionship I would settle for this? Was I so (forgive me for this one) horny I'd take any man to my bed? Was the lady acting like a whore for no other reason than to feel the touch of another?

No, she wasn't. I wiped away the new found tears from my face and admitted what I was doing was hanging on to people who no longer wanted me; and the "why" was no longer important. It was with suddenly clarity through the late night hour I realized not letting go was in essence telling the Almighty He didn't know what He was doing; that I really did know what was better for me than He did.

But, I didn't. I'd listened only half-heartedly to His attempts to tell me to find myself, get myself out of the gutter, get up where I belonged; do that which made me happy, not just paid the bills; but I didn't really believe Him.

I've been told you can't find Mr. Right with Mr. Wrong standing in the way. Wasn't this happening to me now? All these Mr. Wrongs who I thought were Mr. Rights were standing in the way; showing me only part of what was really available to me;

November

leading me down a path that at first looked like the yellow-brick road, but ended up nothing more than a trail of broken glass.

I thought I should feel angry, sad, frustrated; but I didn't. I was … thankful; grateful even for seeing bits and pieces of the type of man I wanted in my life; the type of life I wanted to live; and how I wanted to live it.

Through His design I had been afforded nine weeks of no-school; and no work; a sabbatical of sorts; and right in the middle of this time was my 49th birthday; the beginning of my year of change.

I was given the opportunity to find some direction in my life; all of my life from my work, to my studies, to my family and yes, to the men in my life.

The phone rang again and I did the only thing I could think of; I shut the phone off. I rolled over in bed, whispered a "Thank You" to the Almighty, and then added, "I am listening."

Gratitude
R – Reverence

LIFESTYLE

"You cannot be friends with a king," he said.

"But," I whispered to the nice woman sitting next to me, "what if you're invited?"

She gave me an I-don't-know shrug, the speaker went on to the next participant, and my thoughts stayed behind. I know one must temper the words of another by who the person is; in this case it was a well-known rabbinical speaker from Israel. Although he didn't know everything, he knew a great deal more about being Jewish than I did; hence, it was he and not I who was hosting this session.

This was not the typical Saturday morning service at Temple; this was a special session in which the relationship of the Almighty in our lives was the subject. He did a very good job of explaining the relationship as one of king and servant; not as a slave, but as a trusted staff member. I liked the way he explained it illustrating how very majestic G-d is; how every present He is; and how very respectful we should be when approaching Him.

His reply was answer for my question, "But, what if you consider G-d your friend?"

And yet, there was just something about his matter-of-fact statement which got me to thinking. "Don't kings have friends too?" I asked myself quietly. "Wouldn't it stand to reason that G-d would have His trusted advisors, His close personal relationships, His team that He knew He could always count on to get the job done?"

My questions went unanswered as the topic turned to how to be respectful at Temple and, again, a blanket statement was made stating we don't act the same way in Temple as we do everywhere else. He went on to explain how where we are more reverent, respectful, and wear our best manners in Temple, and we shed this behavior when we reach the Temple doors on our way out.

The only question this brought to mind was, "Who's we??" Without filter, the question passed my lips.

"We, you, me, all of us," he answered. "We don't act the same way out in the world as we do in Temple."

November

"Um, yes, I do." My answer was quiet, but loud enough for him to hear.

"Then you are in the minority," he said and again moved on to the next point.

I'd like to tell you I remember the rest of his talk, the rest of the session; but I can't. What I do remember is leaving their wondering, what is my relationship with the Almighty? I came up with more questions than answers at first; then began to weave my understandings into an answer.

My conclusion is that the Almighty is … well … THE Almighty. As such, He is the provider of all I need; He is the safety and contentment I get out of life; He is my inspiration to be a better person. He has certain rules and ways that He has asked me to live by; and for the most part I do; and when I don't, I ask forgiveness, make amends as I can, and try not to repeat the offense. I respect His ten commandments and as many as I can of His 613; I recognize when I'm eating something not Kosher and do it rarely; I keep the Sabbath; and I do as He asks of me, when He asks and as well as I can.

I take heed of His wants from me to do justice, love mercy, to walk humbly with Him; to love Him, to wait patiently for Him to work in my life and to trust that the piece of Him that passes all understanding will be mine by His love and His mercy.

This is why I was confused by the speaker. Yes, I consider G-d my one and only king; however, He is not as a king in a far away land, ruling by distance and power. He is as a trusted friend, by my side, working with me and through me to get His work done as He sees fit.

And as such, this is not a part-time partnership; a once-in-a-while arrangement; an as-it-suits-my-needs-of-the-moment situation; or a when-it-is-convenient dichotomy. This is a lifestyle; my lifestyle. I am the same person in Temple as I am in my own home, the grocer store, or when I am working. I enter my home the same way I enter the Temple. I can be depended on to be honest and funny and compassionate and loving where ever I am. I am a good friend, a purveyor of doing the right thing, and I treat my G-d as a trusted friend. I accept the gifts He gives me with grace; I turn to Him for advice on everything; I ask for His blessings as the need arises; I depend on His guidance daily, and I am grateful to Him for every single thing in my life.

Gratitude

So, who's right? Is the speaker correct in his opinion of G-d being far and away to be revered and feared; or am I right to believe G-d is a trusted friend, who can count on me to do what is right when it is needed? I don't know the answer to this; I'm almost sure that 100 people will give you 100 different answers which will fall somewhere in between.

All I know is this; my lifestyle works for me; and apparently it works for G-d, else He'd be sure to change it. ☺

A – Amends

November

THE EXTRA MILE

I said I was sorry.

Wasn't that enough?

I'm thinking it isn't; and I'm wondering, where do I go from here? I've done a lot of work to repair the relationships in my life. I've acquired new friends which I share healthy relationships with. I've done the hard work of re-establishing healthy relationships with my siblings, my mom, and some of my other relatives. Of course, I've even done the work to begin a healthy relationship with myself.

If you're about sick of reading the word "healthy" there is a point to it; the person in question was a left-over from my days of "unhealthy" relationships and I was in the process of trying to progress it to a more healthy state.

It was going from bad to worse and I had no idea how to stop it.

I've learned several things about fixing bad relationships; there's a near formula for doing it.

Say you're sorry and mean it.

Make amends as is possible.

Don't do it again.

As simplistic as that sounds, I've found it really does work well; that is, if you know what you are apologizing for, if you know what amends you can make, and if it is behavior you have no intentions of repeating.

In this case, three years had passed since I'd seen him; and as I had changed so very much, and it was safe for me to do so, I said I was sorry for a variety of my actions ... I asked what I could do to make amends ... and I said I wouldn't do it again.

So, why wasn't this working? Why was he yelling at me? Why was he demanding things that I knew would not make it better between us?

The answer was much simpler than I thought it would be. HE hadn't changed. That was not something I had counted on.

I realize to make the transition to a healthy relationship there are a variety of other factors which are involved. It must be safe for me to say I'm sorry – this means I think the odds of me getting hurt by apologizing is low. I must also be sincere in my apology; I can't just say the words. I guess, another part, is I must be respectful in my actions – both towards them and myself.

But, the biggest part is one in which I have no control; they must want to accept my apology. He didn't want my apology. He didn't want to have the relationship changed. He wanted to get what he wanted and would say or do nearly anything to get it. The stumbling block came when I wasn't going to give him what he wanted and he began to revert to controlling and manipulative behavior; in essence, he was throwing a temper tantrum.

My "ouch" reaction came into play when I realized I did the very same thing – not to him – but, to G-d. Sigh. When I didn't get my own way, on my own time table, I started in with the manipulating and controlling behavior. It was not a pretty thing to realize. Fact is it's downright embarrassing to admit.

Who was I to tell the Almighty what was in my best interest? Who was I to demand He do what only He can do so that my bills are paid on time? Who was I to doubt He'd have my back when things were not working out as I'd planned? And to add insult to injury, who was I to turn my back on Him when my life was a mess?

I really hate these lessons sometimes. It's like I was starting out so very pure and holy, so tried and true, so … righteous even, only to realize at some point I'd turned into a whiny cry baby; a Doubting Thomas who expected the Almighty to PROVE Himself to me. Yeah, like I said, not pretty at all.

So, here I sit; one relationship in shambles, the other sitting on the fence waiting for me to do something – something that is, besides bitch and whine and complain to all of my friends. Do something, that is, besides question and doubt and be fearful of the possible loss right around the corner. Do something, that is, besides embarrass myself to all who know me by letting my faith waiver. Double sigh.

There is, however, a solution to both of these problems. It's not the same solution, but still a solution.

The first one, with the friend, is easy – let it go. There really are some relationships that aren't worth having; fact is, they are downright toxic situations in which no matter what you do, the relationship isn't going to get better and you're going to get hurt one way or another.

November

The second one, with the Almighty, is just as easy.
1. Say "I'm sorry" and mean it.
2. Make amends as best as I can.
3. Don't do it again.

And for this one, I'll add just one more:
4. Keep the faith.

I know this process works; I just need to work it. I guess the problem lies in that I am human; as such, I project onto the Almighty the characteristics of those people who have walked in and out of my life. This is not fair for a variety of reasons. The main reason though is G-d is not them and they are not G-d. Yes, they may have tried to convince me that they were; but, they are not.

G-d doesn't want to be them, for He is G-d so why would He? We are His children and it is my hope that He understands that only He is perfect and I've got a lot of amends to make to Him by going the extra mile. The first is to stop worrying about the things I cannot control – that's His job. He does it very well. I think I'll let Him.

Gratitude
C – Charity

GIVING BACK

It was only seven dollars.

But, they weren't mine.

I had decided today was the perfect day to stay inside; and for good reason. It was one of those cold, rainy/snowy, windy spring days that remind you that winter is not yet over. As it was Sunday to boot, it was a wonderful luxury to not go to my Hebrew class and instead, to relax, color my hair, do some reading, and play video games.

Yet, dinner time was looming, and although I'd set chicken in the fridge to defrost, I really didn't feel like cooking. With a sly grin, I decided pizza, for the third time this week, would be the order of the day. Thirty minutes and seventeen dollars later, I had a piping hot pizza and a two-liter of soda on my countertop just waiting for me to dig in. So, I did.

Imagine my surprise when I returned to the kitchen, moved the pizza box to the fridge and found seven dollars on my counter top. I looked at it in amazement; I didn't have any fives on me tonight, and all the ones I had were in the jar. It took me a few minutes, but I decided that the only one who'd even been near my flat, was the pizza delivery guy. Somehow the money must have stuck to the bottom of the box, and it must have been transferred when I put the box on the counter.

There was no other option in my mind; I called the pizza shop and talked to the delivery guy telling him I had the money, and I'd be here all night for him to come and pick it up. It was then that he said something unusual. "I knew I had more change then I could find; you're a real lifesaver."

It was only seven dollars. But when he picked it up, he repeated his gratitude and said, "I was just telling my wife that I didn't know where I'd lost it at and didn't know how I was going to replace it." He looked away for a minute, and then looked back. "You know, not a lot of people would have done this; they wouldn't have called me. They would have just kept the money."

I said the only thing I could think of, "It wasn't mine."

He said his thanks again as I gave him the cash, and he left.

November

It was only seven dollars; or was it? To me it was extra cash that showed up on my counter. To him, however, it was money he didn't have; and furthermore, money that could have cost him his job. Companies don't much care for employees losing their money.

I recalled a time when I didn't know where I was going to come up with the money for a pack of cigarettes; and here I had his money. It was his money; I gave no thought of keeping it.

It was some time later that my friend, who had been over the night before, asked me if I'd moved the breakfast tray. I said I had, and relayed the story of the new pizza guy. It was then that he told me HE had put the money there thinking I wouldn't have accepted it had he offered. I didn't know how to feel; I was conflicted. Thinking it was the pizza guy's money, I felt good about giving it back. Knowing it was my friend's gift to me, I felt badly for giving it to someone else.

Then it dawned on me, how could the pizza guy be short the amount that I had found?? It didn't take a huge leap to believe that someone else had shorted him, and this made up for it.

When we keep something that doesn't belong to us, it's not just stealing it's tarnishing whatever is associated with it. When we give to another with no thought of getting it back, it makes it extra special. But, sometimes, just sometimes, I think it's a matter of just giving it back.

Gratitude
E – Excitement

THE SEARCH FOR IT

I thought it was a matter of patience.

I was mistaken.

As I've always believed I've had the patience of a two-year old, it came as quite the surprise to realize it wasn't the patience I had; it was the attention span.

Wanting something, and wanting it right NOW, and acting like a spoiled brat when I didn't get it were all signs (or so I thought) of being impatient. So the other day, I was thinking about why I feel this need to get my own way, and expect certain things in my life to work, all the while wanting them to work RIGHT NOW.

I recognized a pattern in my life. I found something I wanted; I'd go after IT with great abandonment and excitement; I'd get IT and be happy; or I wouldn't get IT and be angry, frustrated, depressed, or any combination of the aforementioned. Either way, if I got IT or I didn't, the emotions would fade; either I'd be content for a bit or I'd be in a bad state for a bit.

Oddly enough, it didn't matter what the IT was, the pattern was the same. IT could be a good grade at university; a new client or a new job; a new man or an old one revisited; or a new car, new furniture, a new outfit, a new ... something.

Why? What was my fascination with the new and improved? Yes, I did cherish the fact my furnishings, my car, my clothing were all the trappings of the lifestyle I'd created and they all 'fit' into what I deemed I wanted my lifestyle to be; and I've no desire to replace anything I have.

So, why is it that I am on this search for the ever elusive, IT? And just as importantly, why the driven need to have whatever IT is, right now?

Was this a matter of:

Feeling I was entitled to IT because I had worked for IT?

Knowing I deserved IT as I was a "good person"?

Not trusting all involved for IT to come to fruition if it wasn't done right now?

Being afraid I would lose whatever IT was and be the lesser for it?

November

Or most likely, knowing myself well enough to know if I didn't get what ever I wanted, I'd just move on to the next IT and go from there?

I've often said the only constant in my life is change; this could be something as simple as getting a different fountain pen or as drastic as moving 250 miles, alone. Was this search for the IT just part of my drive for the need for change? Was it that I was missing something in my life and I thought getting IT would make me complete? Could it be to not search for this IT meant I was settling for second best? Or, could it just mean I'm always looking, searching, for something else to fill my life with to feel like a contributing member of society?

My mother was one who would constantly describe me, to anyone who'd listen, as being very "high-strung"; she was fond of saying, "That girl just can't sit still; it's like she's got ants in her pants or something."

Or something. Hmm. I wonder what that something is – and if I'll ever find IT. The search and the excitement of the chase … continues.

SUMMARY

As you focused on GRACE this month, did you see a parallel to an issue in your own life? The following ten questions may help you gain new perspective on how to manage it.

Questions to ponder:

1. Is this issue bigger than me?

2. What is my part in resolving the issue?

3. Is now the right time?

4. What's stopping me?

5. How do I remove the barriers?

6. What resources will I need to get started?

7. What resources do I have?

November

Answers to Act on:

8. What isn't working?

9. What is working?

10. What's the next step?

To do List:

Gratitude

December

MIRACLES

December is a month of miracles. The true beauty of a miracle is that it happens in times of great chaos, catastrophe or confusion; and they make things right. Sometimes the miracle is in seeing all the things in our life that aren't working and getting the incredible strength and courage to make the hard decisions to change them. During this time of upheaval, focus on …

G   for GLORY
R   for REALITY
A   for ABSOLUTION
C   for CHANGE
E   for EXTREME

HOLIDAY MIRACLES

I'll not be decorating for the holidays this year.

That's what I told my kids.

They were shocked; they were stunned; they were speechless even. It was a very rare moment. When they regained their voices they bombarded with me with the usual responses of how I *had* to decorate my patio for the annual apartment complex competition; I *had* to hang my little tree from the ceiling to shine through the half-moon window; I *had* to decorate my white six-footer in red lights; because to do otherwise would mean it just wasn't Christmas.

No. I didn't *have* to do any of those things. Just as importantly, I didn't WANT to do any of those things. I had fallen into a funk I didn't know how to get out of; and decorating for no other reason than because someone else thought it was necessary just wasn't in my plan. I mean, for crying out loud, no one was coming to my home for the holidays, so, why bother?

"Please, mama, please," my youngest son pleaded, "you've got to decorate – you ALWAYS decorate! It's just not Christmas if you don't decorate." He didn't seem to understand what kind of anti-holiday funk I'd fallen into. "You go get into your jammies, watch *How the Grinch Stole Christmas*, the cartoon version, *It's a Wonderful Life*, AND THEN *Miracle on 34th Street*, cry your eyes out and soon you'll be bouncing around your flat decorating up a storm. You'll see, mama, you'll feel the holiday miracles, I promise." Ahhh, the hopefulness of the young; if only I could find it again. But, he just didn't understand.

My ex-husband had made Thanksgiving dinner so unbearable for all of us that we decided to have a family holiday party at my youngest son's house the Saturday before Christmas. This way here, all four families involved could spend the actual day with their individual families and no one would have to put up with the tension exhibited at Thanksgiving.

The problem was – although I'd be driving home Christmas Eve day – I had no individual family; I just had … me … and the cat. It was the first Christmas of my life where I would be … alone.

December

If there was going to be no one there but me, why bother decorating?

I had mixed feelings about being alone on Christmas. I liked the idea of some of the lesser liked members of my family not being at my home; but, oh, how I missed the children – especially as this would be my youngest grand daughter's first holiday. I resolved myself to spending the day as a volunteer at the hospital. This was the best use of my time, all things considered.

Then there was also the issue of money. December is my poor month – always has been, I'm guessing it always will be. This December wasn't my worse one, but wasn't one of my better ones either; rent was paid and the utilities were still on because I had cashed in an insurance annuity and got a major student loan refund. There was nothing left over for a holiday celebration. Fact was I didn't really know where I was going to come up with the money for the gas just to get to the family party. I had to break this funk!

I decorated my patio.

I bought an angel with the money that I got by returning things I was going to return anyway as they were things I didn't need.

I put up my tree – but – with the lights and only two little boxes of bulbs.

And I ... hoped.

Then I met a man – a hero if you will – who through a general conversation said he had some really good tickets to a football game that he wasn't going to attend, so was looking to sell them. The game was on Christmas Eve day. He said it was the Rams vs. the Washington Redskins. Hmm. My oldest son loved the Redskins; his wife was a Rams fan. Could I use this as an excuse to get their family to my home for the holiday? More urgently, could I come up with the $130 to make it happen?

Now, normally $130 doesn't mean a whole lot to me; especially as I'm used to dropping $100 to get my hair cut. But, in December, just $20 can make all the difference; this year was no exception. I'd won $167 at the craps table with a friend of mine. I saved $100 for the trip to the family party; I spent $43 of those dollars on the meds for my cat; I had $24 left.

I borrowed $60 – which I didn't use right away, thought I'd save it for my backup.

Miracles

I won second place in the patio competition and received $75.

I got a holiday card from my mother that was so wonderful it made me cry – surprise number one; with a check for $75 – surprise number two. I spent it all on gifts for the kids.

And I bought the tickets; *and* agree to pay the $28 for my youngest son's new cell phone, *and* listened to the voice in the back of my mind showing me where to get the video game for my grandson; *and* picked up the baby doll that giggled when you pressed its tummy for my oldest granddaughter along with the porcelain tea set; *and* the Lilly learning doll for my youngest granddaughter. *And* then … I found the extra stash of $20 to pay for the gift certificate for my youngest son's girlfriend, my cigarettes, and some cat food.

And oddly enough, I realized something; I realized miracles aren't always big things like someone who is dying who lives; or car crash victims walking away from the accident; or any of the millions of things that flood the news every day. Miracles can also be the little things; an unexpected check for $75 that made a difference; the hearing about tickets that mean more than just a game; or a cell phone that has all the bells and whistles being on sale; or finding just the right thing for just the right person at just the right time, or the unexpected way a funk lifts from your shoulders when you see all of these miracles.

Miracles can be just a simple Hallmark card from your mom that says: "So now, when you might need it most, may you find returned to you, the warm support of others, till your days are brighter, too." Signed, <u>Love</u> <u>you</u> <u>lots</u>, Mother.

Yep, miracles happen every day in the big ways; but more importantly in the little ways as well.

R – Reality

THROUGH THE EYES OF A CHILD

My chairs are really comfortable.
I have bad hair days.
This is all according to my oldest grand daughter. She's right, my chairs are really comfortable, and when I wake up first thing in the morning, I am having a bad hair day.

My life had gotten beyond the point of frustration; I was at the end of my rope, and my nerves were shot. So, I asked my oldest son how much it would cost for him to bring his three kids up for the weekend. It was truly the best $100 I've ever spent.

Needless to say with my recent travel history, I was terrified that something "bad" would happen. I also went to see my doctor before they arrived on Friday. 'Tis true my nerves are directly related to my stomach; but it didn't explain the horrible nausea just after eating, the terrible stabbing pains in the stomach, and the further down "gut pain" as my doctor put it. Food poisoning, however, did explain it all.

So between my nerves, the terror of something "bad" happening, and the food poisoning, I about cried when my granddaughter hugged me, whispered she missed me into my ear, and became my shadow for two days.

It was through her and her sister that I learned a lot about my life; things I wouldn't even have really noticed. For example, my house is "really, really" clean, my bed covers are soft, my bed is really comfortable—though it's not really good for jumping on. I tell the "best" stories, I cook really good mac and cheese, and I'm a really good mother.

That last point was bittersweet. When my youngest granddaughter started calling me "mother," well, I wasn't sure how to take it. I'm still not all that sure. I realized that I am a good mother. I give hugs and kisses for boo-boos; I allow a little chocolate after a good dinner; I don't mind cartoons if it's at rest after playing outside. There's also the habit I have of never breaking a "pinkie-promise."

My grandchildren showed me just how trustworthy I am; how I only yell when I'm "really, really scared and want me to stop in my tracks." They don't have to ask to sit in my lap, do have to ask to drink my coffee, and NEVER have to think twice to get a hug and kiss. They can play with anything in the house, never touch my cigarettes unless they are handing them to me, and only my oldest is allowed in my purse.

I'm fun, I keep them safe, I can be trusted, and the tickle monster is only a quick second away; I like to play ball, romp on the monkey bars, and give horsey-rides around the pool. I can be trusted to be there when they need me, cuddle any time, and listen.

I expect the best from them, and they from me, and each gives the other what is expected.

So, why is it then that I don't see my life, see me, the way they do?

What if I did?

What if I stopped being afraid of what "might" happen and know that I step up to the plate when it "does" happen? Why do I fear the unknown when I know if a child falls into the pool, I'm quick to pull them out? If they are broken, I'm quick to either fix it or try my best to fix it?

Maybe, just maybe, it is no longer a matter of me being afraid of not doing the right thing, of not being able to cope with the situation, of being afraid of doing more harm than good, but in realizing how painful it is for me to see them in pain and still do the right thing.

I was at dinner a few days ago with a good friend of mine, and while we were discussing the kids coming up, I told her how afraid I was. I reminded her how in the last six months there has not been a person in my immediate family that I have not come to the aid of, all the accidents, and all the ER visits, when she said something strange.

She said, "You were the rescuer; you were the one they trusted to do the right thing."

"I don't think so," I said, "as every time I walked into their room or went to their side, they broke out crying."

"That proves my point," she said. "The minute they saw you, they knew they were safe; they knew you would make it all right; they knew they could now cry and didn't have to be brave anymore. Children," she continued, "can be brave beyond their years; but, when they see their hero, their rescuer, they know it's okay; it's now safe to cry. They don't have to be strong anymore, because you are there."

I hope she's right; but I hope to not have to prove it anymore. It hurts to see those I love in pain; it hurts to know there is sometimes little I can do about it, but it helps to know I didn't cause any of it.

Odd as it sounds, there is a part of me that is grateful—grateful I was there to comfort, support, and make the tough decisions for my family. It hurts to see them in pain, and I hope that I don't have to do it again. But, if I do, I know that I can and will do what is right. I don't need to fear that aspect of it anymore as I've proven time and again that I am strong enough to cope with it all.

I know I was there for them, made things easier for them; I just hope that this bad patch is over, the lesson is learned, and there are great days ahead of us.

I wish that I could have my granddaughter's faith that no matter what happens, it will all be okay. I think she's given me a bit of it on this trip; she was my rescuer. She is the one teaching me what true faith is. She is the one who gets up every morning, enjoys all the good things that are going on in her life, and knows I'll be there to make things right.

As she turns to me, I turn to the Almighty. As I am her hero, G-d is mine; He will always have my back, make right what is wrong, will kiss the boo-boos in my life, and make them all better.

Miracles
A – Absolution

CLOSING THE BOOK

My home book collection rivals some small libraries.

So, why am I closing—actually considering burning—a book?

I received a poisoned text message today from the last guy I dated. It arrived only because he wanted to see me again, and I said no. His response escalated into a tirade about how many intimate details he knew about my life to prove himself and ended with him calling me several unpleasant names. After reading this, two things happened. The first is I got a call from someone considering him for a job looking for his cell number. I gave them his number. The second was I realized part of what he said was right; I based how well someone knew me on if they knew my 'intimate' details.

I've spent the majority of my life trying to figure out my past: writing the book on the events that have colored who I am. But, yesterday when I was talking with my new guy he said something strange. He said, "It doesn't matter what you've done; for no matter how bad it was, it made you who you are today. Let's start today and just live with who we are, not who we were."

He has a point. I don't like his point, but he does have one. I guess I don't like his point because I feel for someone to know who I am, it is important for them to know who I've been, as the poisoned text message confirmed. I realize now that I'm wrong.

I also realize that:

- It doesn't matter what events made me strong, or smart, or kind, or adventuresome, just that I am.
- What hurts made me honest, trustworthy, or humble do not matter; it only matters that I am.
- It is of little value to know how I raised my children, or the children that I acquired, just that I'm good with kids.
- What my ex-husband – equally so the men I've dated – has or has not done really has no impact on my current or future relationships.

Certainly there are events of my life which are humorous or tragic that show strength or weakness, make me look good and not so good. They are mine and mine alone. I'm beginning to realize

December

that is the *only* value they hold. They are how I define who I am. They are the reasons which justify my actions. But, is sharing them really NECESSARY? I'm beginning to think not.

I told some one recently, after reading their e-mail response to another, that this wasn't a court of law; they didn't have to justify their actions or feelings; what they were writing was a simple reply to someone, not the Enlightenment of the French Revolution.

And that's when the poisoned text message really hit home. Isn't that what I do? When someone asks me about my kids, I go into a long drawn out history of them instead of just saying that I have two sons? Or when someone asks me where I'm from, I get into a detailed account of my travel history, instead of just saying I've bounced around for a bit and then landed in St. Louis? Or when someone asks me for my help I site an example from my past to make a point instead of just giving them the help they wanted.

I was embarrassed by my actions; my self-imposed arrogance; my ego-driven methods of communication which didn't enhance relationships, but instead destroyed them. I wasn't adding to the experience; I was seen as desperately selling myself—of trying to paint a picture of my own worth that didn't come off as sharing but could be seen as intimidating, or worse yet, arrogant.

I've said a million times, "Perception very rarely has anything to do with the truth." Yet, I'm just now realizing that when I give my past experiences they are, in effect, building the perception of who I am, not giving the picture of who I've become.

Today. It is all we have control over; it is built on the foundation of all of our yesterdays; and colored by the hope of all of our tomorrows. So it is today that I close the book on all of my yesterdays; and in doing so, giving myself absolution; freeing myself from the blame or guilt over past wrongs that I can't change and releasing myself from the consequences, obligations and penalties I've already paid.

There is a welcomed freedom with absolution; one we can give to another, and more importantly, one we give to ourselves.

Miracles
C – Change

NEW HABITS

He expected me to yell at him.
I surprised us both and didn't.
It wasn't so much that I condoned my youngest son winding up in jail; it was more a matter of me not feeling it was my place to tell him it was wrong of him to do so. It was my place to come up with the bail money, but, that was my choice.

Perhaps I should back up. Last night, as I was just sitting down to enjoy yet another of my Judaism classes, my son's girlfriend called me. Her first words were, "Your son's in jail."

Not believing what I was hearing, I said, "What?" It wasn't a matter of anger, just confusion.

She repeated herself, and I excused myself from the class. Over the course of the next few minutes I was informed that he needed $120 within the hour to raise bail, else it was going to be $300. It was an act of G-d that I actually HAD the $120, but I couldn't get it to her within the hour.

A quick call to my other son and a few other calls to this and that resulted in my son getting out of jail. We circled the family wagons, as it were, pooled our resources, and all was well. Throughout it all, I had not screamed, raised my voice, or broken down into sobs. I did falter a little bit, but only for a moment.

Now that the "crisis" had been handled, what, if anything, was I going to do about his actions? Hmm.

Past practice would dictate that I would get myself to a place where I could discuss this situation with him in-depth; in other words, I'd go home so I could call him up just to scream at him, berate him, infuse into him the importance of paying a speeding ticket BEFORE the warrant is issued, and the overall ills of speeding in the first place.

The reality was I no longer subscribed to past practice. What I did was go back and finish my two-hour class, stopped by the local retail store on my way home and wired his girlfriend the money to pay her grandfather back the bail money he'd fronted her. When I called to let her know I had sent the money, my son (who by this time was now home) answered her phone. I asked if she were

December

there, he said yes, to which I calmly replied, "May I speak with her?" He was shocked, stunned, nearly speechless even.

"Sure," he said, "since you don't want to talk to ME!"

"Not now, little one," I calmly said. "Not now."

He handed the phone to her, and we discussed her getting the money. I was calm, cool, collected even, and ended the conversation by telling her I loved her and to call me when she had gotten the money.

It took me nearly an hour to call him back. And when I did, he was still stunned.

"Hey, baby. How ya doing?" I asked him, my voice denoting that I was not angry or upset, but actually in a good mood.

"How do you THINK I'm doing when my own mother won't speak to me?" He was on the verge of tears.

"It's not so much that I *wouldn't* speak to you," I calmly said, "it was more a matter of it not being the right time to speak to you. I needed to get myself together; I needed to deal with this in my own way; and I didn't want to say anything that I would later regret."

"You could have said anything!" he exclaimed. "You know I would have forgiven you later!"

"Ah," I replied, "that's not the point. It was not YOUR forgiveness I was seeking; it was my own. And I didn't want to say anything that I would have to apologize for later."

He didn't understand, and it was scaring him in the process. Never in his life had I been so calm and cool and not later blew up at him. Again, past practice dictated that once the crisis was averted, I'd come unglued. It was not the case now.

I had changed. It wasn't the type of change that we give lip service to by saying, "Next time, I'll do it this way." No, this WAS the next time; this WAS the way I was handling it. I probably could have handled it differently, better still than what I did. After all, no one ASKED me for the bail money; I just presumed that when his girlfriend called me, the act in itself WAS asking for the money. I could have NOT reached out to my oldest son and gotten him involved; after all, the end result had nothing to do with him. But, he was the one I turned to in times of family crisis and to NOT do so would have been too far outside of the family dynamics for anyone's comfort. My oldest son expects me to call him in times of family crisis; he feels it's his position to help as he can; and he takes a great deal of pride in my turning to him. Some things don't need to change; they are good as they stand.

The Almighty showed me how to spot manipulative behavior in others, how to stand strong against it, and how to refrain from propagating the practice. Now He's giving me the opportunity to relate this to my children in a manner that is good for all of us.

But what is really the heart of this issue? The only word that comes to mind is control. My control over issues in my son's life; and I am embarrassed.

This is not a new issue, just the most recent one. I had acted on impulse when he told me last week he lost his phone; my instinct was to get him a new one. I acted on impulse when I called the cell phone carrier and told them his phone wasn't turned back on and started the process to have it done. I didn't ask him if he wanted me to get him a new phone, or even have his phone turned on. I presumed he did want all of these things and just did them—no thought process whatsoever. And maybe that is the key.

When faced with the bail out situation, I took a moment or two to think. I presumed that he didn't want to spend the night in jail, and I concurred that I didn't WANT him to spend the night in jail either. But at what point is it my Mommy-duty, and at what point is it not my business? Where is the line between stepping up to the plate and interfering?

I don't know for sure. But I do know that the outlying issues regarding the cell phone and the knee-jerk reaction of coming up with the bail money just felt right. I'm proud of myself for not resorting to manipulative and condescending behavior over why he was in jail in the first place. I'm proud that I took the high road and only helped a little bit, not controlling the whole situation; and especially NOT expecting something in return for my help. I did what I did, because I thought it was the right thing to do.

Additionally, I didn't do what I've done in the past because I thought it would be wrong. I realized I did not have control over his life, his decisions, or his choices; I do, however, have control over mine. Maybe the growth has to do with determining where those boundaries lie and then letting go of the control.

December

E – Extreme

VISIBLE CHANGES

I saw the office building today from my flat window.

It's the first sign that winter is nearly upon us.

Like magic, in the spring time, the building starts to disappear as the foliage between us sprouts its leaves. Equally so, it reappears when the leaves fall. But, this is not the only change I've seen this week. Last weekend, I got the idea that I need to work on cleaning up my credit report so I've been getting the information I need to do this. My divorce papers have been filed and will be served this next week. I signed my teaching contract for next semester this past Monday and dropped one of my master's classes so as to be in a better position to succeed.

So, here I sit; with the trappings of my life all about me, and I whisper, "Is this all there is?" For three years I've struggled to get to this point—a time when my bills are paid on time with a bit left over, a time when I can be free of a marriage that wasn't good; a time when I'm surrounded by friends and family members who are trustworthy; a time when my emotional health could be described as "stable". I've worked very smart to do well at a job that makes a difference, to find a program of study that feeds the passion I have for learning, and to keep a lifestyle that reflects who I am, what I value and the social level I have attained.

There are little changes as well; I've finally gotten a new laptop that I bought just for me, for no other reason than I've wanted one for so very long. I stood up for myself with my education and made a compromise that not only respected myself, but also was one I could become passionate over. I find that I'm living a life of righteousness when I do and say things in a manner that I don't have to apologize for later. And there are boundaries: ones that I am setting, ones that I am recognizing and respecting. I'm learning how to feel feelings and still act in a way that is acceptable; in a nutshell, I am recognizing that I can be angry, upset, hurt, frustrated, and yes, even sometimes depressed, but that is no excuse for bad behavior. Nor am I accepting these excuses to justify other's bad behavior as well. I'm also learning that just because someone else believes a certain way doesn't mean that it is more acceptable than the way I believe.

I realize these are extreme changes for me, especially when I remember there was a point in my life where if someone told me to do something, I would do it without question, believing they knew what was best. I would value someone else's opinion or wants over my own.

Now that I think about it, it's rather like the trees that sit between my flat and the office building next door. Their effect on my life changes with the seasons; sometimes hiding who I am, sometimes making me more visible; sometimes coloring my world, sometimes cutting me bare; but whether a complement or a deterrent, I can't control them.

But just like those trees, I need to stand strong, weathering the storms, enjoying the sunshine, and realizing that no matter what, I am exactly where I belong.

December

SUMMARY

As you focused on GRACE this month, did you see a parallel to an issue in your own life? The following ten questions may help you gain new perspective on how to manage it.

Questions to ponder:

1. Is this issue bigger than me?

2. What is my part in resolving the issue?

3. Is now the right time?

4. What's stopping me?

5. How do I remove the barriers?

6. What resources will I need to get started?

7. What resources do I have?

Miracles
Answers to Act on:

8. What isn't working?

9. What is working?

10. What's the next step?

To do List:

January

PLANNING

January is a month of planning. Now that you've assessed, given thanks, and witnessed miracles, it's time to begin finding ways to implement those discoveries! During this time of transition, focus on …

      G   for GOALS
      R   for REAL
      A   for AWAKENINGS
      C   for COMFORT
      E   for ENVIRONMENT

Planning
G – Goals

SPRING PLANTING

"You reap what you sow."
What??
Being a city girl at heart, I didn't get it. Oh, sure I understood you were responsible for your actions, and I understood if you did good things, good things would come back to you. But, up until recently, I didn't understand that it also meant you have to *SOW* something to *REAP* something.

Or, in other words, you have to plant a seed in the garden of your life if you expect anything to grow.

Now that sounds pretty lofty, I realize, but, I started to imagine what my garden would really look like; what would be in it and what wouldn't be. To do that, I first had to start with my crops—my priorities if you will.

I told someone recently that G-d was not a priority in my life; He WAS my life; He colored every aspect of my life. It wasn't a matter of saying, "Okay, number three on my list is, 'What am I going to do for G-d today?'" It was a matter of looking at every aspect of my life and figuring out how to best serve G-d in each of those aspects and how to best use the gifts He gave me.

In the garden of my life, He would be the soil. All things would then be planted in His soil medium.

So, in my garden of life, what are my crops?

Me: The things I do for myself to nurture my soul, enhance my life, maintain my emotional, mental, and physical well-being; financial support for myself with the goal to be secure; the acts and words I give to others to hopefully enhance their lives along the way; and what I give back to my community, my world.

My work: That's a tough one as I've just recently started to change careers. I read recently that the transition from one career to another takes about six months, and can take up to a year or more. This made me feel really good as I didn't feel like I was flailing quite so badly but was actually making good progress in this arena.

My studies: With only one term left before my research project and graduation, this is a short term priority. That is, until I

January

decide to go back to school again. This area still needs some tending as this next term I'm retaking a class that I had failed.

My family and friends: This is a really cool area as I've done so much work in the past year. The relationships I have are strong and only need some minor maintenance to flourish. Two years ago I couldn't say this. I've finally gotten to the point where I know which family members I can turn to and which are wise to avoid. I've two "best" friends, a new friend who's quickly becoming another "best" friend, and the rest, well, the rest really weren't friends to begin with. I took the lessons these people had to give me, gave back what I could, and let them go.

Significant other: I have realized when this area of my life is in at least a loose order the other areas work very well. Currently, this area of my life is under a severe thunderstorm watch; but in the meantime, I'm learning lessons, as to how to grow a healthy relationship.

So now that I my crops are planted, what do I have to do to make them grow, flourish, and produce a good harvest? Planting a seed every day in each area is a good start. But, as any good farmer will tell you, planting isn't enough. You also have to water, feed, till the soil, and let's not forget pulling out the weeds.

The hardest part of weeding is recognizing the weeds from new plant growth. For me, the best way to recognize the difference is to figure out what I want the finished garden to contain. To do this, I need to examine the garden and ask , "What would my life look like if it were my perfect garden?"

What determines what a weed is, and what's a wildflower that is only adding to the beauty of the garden? I would guess it would be whether its addition is sapping the garden of its energy or if it is adding to the overall well being of the garden. Those items that are not focused on increasing the health of the garden, well, no matter how pretty they are, they need to be removed.

Add to this garden the weather of life. Sure, some days are sunny and warm; but other days are cloudy, windy, and rainy; let's not forget the early frost. Those are the minor things we have to deal with. But, what about the really big stuff? What about the torrential down pours, the hard frosts, the unexpected snow storms? What do we do when one area of our garden is damaged or worse yet, nearly wiped out?

Planning

As any good gardener will tell you, at that point, you salvage what you can and start over. You replant the seeds in the fertile soil, you till and water and feed, and, you pray for good weather.

We don't live in a greenhouse where we can be protected by the elements, where we are watered and fed according to someone else's schedule, where our soil is the medium of man, and where our harvests may be many, but they are lacking nutrients.

We live in the real world where we know it is the SOIL that sustains our garden; and for all of our hardships, for all of our beatings from the elements, the crops are stronger and the fruit of that harvest is rich and sweet and nourishing to the soul.

R – Real

IMPOSTERS

I know all about imposters.

I am one.

I wish I had a dollar for every time I've said, "Don't buy into the perception of who you think I am and believe that you know me." I've said it to nearly every man I've ever dated.

If you look at my life, you will find I live in a nice place, decorated as I see fit; I drive a decent car, dress well for every occasion, exhibit a high level of social grace, and have done some really remarkable things in my life. I've gotten a good education, have some ambitious goals, and hold tightly to some pretty wonderful dreams.

The feeling of being an imposter comes when I realize I have all the trappings of a good and successful life, but, it is a hollow existence as I've no one to share it with. So, I get up every morning and continue with the charade. I go to work, I look for opportunities that the Almighty offers me, I do the best I can to take care of myself. Looking from the outside in, my life looks pretty good.

The reality is I live in a very pretty prison; it's an empty, hollow, very lonely existence. I've stopped telling people not to buy into the perception of who I am because they are going to think whatever they want to think, and it's not my job to tell them what to do or believe.

It is my job, however, to take care of myself, to use the gifts the Almighty has given me wisely, to help those I can as I am able, and to become the best I can. No one, however, said I had to like it.

So, why do I think that the feelings I have right now have PERMANENT stamped on them? I don't know. I'm just trying to find my way, trying to find some happiness in my life, and trying, above all, to feel loved.

Henry Wadsworth Longfellow is quoted as saying, "We judge ourselves by what we feel capable of doing, while others judge us by what we have already done." Maybe that is where the discrepancies lie; we judge ourselves on possible future outcomes, others judge us by past performance. We deem all that we have acquired as *normal*; where others deem all that we have acquired as *extraordinary*. We see where we are in life as below where our promise dictates we should be; others just see where we are as where they would like to be.

But, they don't see the whole picture like we do. We see our financial status and know we are just one paycheck away from being homeless; they don't see the fear we live with everyday. They see our well-dressed selves as making a fashion statement; we know we bought the clothes at a discount outlet for what they would pay at a retail store for a lower quality. They see our cars and think they are paid for; we know we are two months behind in the payments and days away from repossession. They experience our social graces and believe them to be sign of good-breeding; they don't realize it is the mask we hide behind for fear of our true selves being discovered.

And part of us envies them. They have the solid marriage, the loving relationships, the time to spend with their family and friends. It is not that we are too busy to spend time with our family and friends it's that we don't HAVE any. We sit alone with no one to talk to or share with or enjoy. We envy them for their belief about who we are, fully aware if they knew the truth about us, they would not want to be with us let alone BE us. We strive to become the person they see in us, ever wary that we may never become that person; ever fearful that they will discover some horrible, horrible truth about us. What is that truth? Is it that we are living a lie? Is it that we are really not who they THINK we are? Or is it, maybe, just maybe, that we can't see us as they do, and there is no horrible truth to discover. Fact is there is nothing they could discover that could change their mind about us.

What if we could see us through their eyes? Would that be such a bad thing? Would it be such a terrible thing if we could—for just a little while—see the good person others see in us? What if we could believe all the things others believe about us? And what if we could see the value in us that they see? Could we stop discounting all of the gifts that we have to offer? Could we accept that others see us as kind, loving, smart, and pretty; and, maybe, just maybe, as a valuable companion?

Would we be believing a lie or would we just take a moment from our loneliness and rejoice in the wonderful people we are? What if we bought into their perception of who we are and then lived that perception? Would it be a sin to think of only our good

January

qualities while trying to work on our bad? Would it be wrong to forget, for just a little while, the heavy load of guilt we carry for all the woulda, shoulda, couldas in our life? Would we be lying to ourselves or would we finally be able to see who we really are?

I'd like to become the person others see me as. I'd like others to see themselves as I see them. But most of all, I'd like to be true to myself, and if living the perception is the first step, then I'm already there.

They say to know another you need to walk a mile in their shoes. Perhaps to know our true selves we need to see ourselves with the loving eyes of those closest to us.

Planning
A – Awakenings

CYCLES

I called my mother yesterday.

It was the third time this week.

The first time was to just shoot the breeze; the second was to borrow a few dollars; and the third ... well ... the third time found me in a meltdown needing comfort.

My mother will be the first to admit she and I don't have a greeting card type of relationship; I'd agree with her. Our relationship has been turbulent at best, toxic at worst. So, why is it, do you think, that when I'm in the middle of a meltdown, the first person I want to talk to is my mother?

I don't know; I do know that for all of the crap we put each other through and all of the games we used to play, there comes a phone call in which she puts everything aside and talks *to* me. There is this person my mother becomes when I'm in meltdown that makes me glad she IS my mother.

She doesn't discount me or my accomplishments; she NEVER says, "I told you so," and she'd walk barefoot through hot coals before she'd say, "How dumb can you be??" No, that's not my mother.

My mother is British; period. She carries this ever present dignity—this stiff-upper-lip style, and the you-can-do-anything-you-set-your-mind-to attitude. It's almost insulting the way she looks at me as if I'm the village idiot and says, "How can you possibly NOT believe in yourself??" Then she'll take another drag on another of her too many for the day cigarettes, and say, "You ALWAYS come out good. No matter what it is you come out on top! You could fall into a bucket of you-know-what and come out fresh as a daisy."

Then she'll get a bit indignant and say, "How dare you not believe in MY oldest daughter? That's just unacceptable!" She refuses to believe that I can't do something. It's not that her beliefs are ill-founded for I have time and again gotten myself out of a sticky situation; it's more a matter of when confronted with said situations, the doubts creep up and jump on my back – HARD. Then the cycle of fear, anger, and then determination begins, and the situation is resolved.

January

So why is it, do you think, that I feel the need to go through the fear and anger before I resolve the problem? Perhaps it's just a bad habit; maybe it is necessary to get me to my "thinking" spot; or maybe, just maybe it is the mechanism I use to justify my abilities of getting myself out of those situations. It seems to me that stopping to think before reacting (i.e. letting fear and anger take over) would be a much simpler way of solving problems; there'd certainly be less drama.

Which begs the question, do I really NEED the drama to feel? Is my life so very hollow (or shallow) that I need the extra drama just to get the brain cells in motion; to get the juices flowing; to get me up off my butt to get the job done? I really, REALLY hope not. For if this truly is the case, there will never be a time when I can solve one of life's problems without the drama. Is this the way I really want to live? I think not.

So, what then is the solution to break this cycle? Let's take a step back and see what caused this apex in the first place.

Believe it or not, it was the fact that I didn't have five dollars for a pack of cigarettes. I know it seems like a minor thing in comparison to the worry of the worlds; but this was the straw that not only broke said camel's back, but was the FINAL straw in a long litany of financial woes.

I must admit I'd been getting hints along the way that my financial situation was the weakest link in my life chain; but I didn't think it was THAT BAD of a problem. Fact was I didn't think my financial situation WAS a problem. It was an annoyance, yes; a problem, not really; a lifestyle, most definitely. I figured the ebb and flow, the highs and lows, were the price I paid for living a non-conventional lifestyle. I've lived the last 23 years of my life wondering where my next paycheck was coming from and with the belief that if I was on the right path G-d would provide.

And He did.

(He didn't stop now, in case you're wondering.)

But, it was no longer ENOUGH. Living from one check to the next had been a thorn in my side for as long as I can remember. However, it's been an open festering sore since November 2006 when I closed my business. I believe my teaching job last year was a G-d send; and it was. However, I started looking at my paycheck … differently.

Planning

Instead of thinking of it as a foundation to build on; I thought of it as my ONLY source of income. What started out to be a comfort has now become my limitation.

As I said, I'd been getting hints along the way, but I brushed them aside, not realizing these hints were adding up to a two-by-four between the eyes: the same two-by-four which instilled the fear, anger, and then the determination.

About two months ago I took one of those on-line quizzes to figure out how "balanced" my life was. On a scale of one to 25 (with 25 being the highest/best) this quiz graded six areas of my life. I must admit I was rather pleased to realize five of the six areas scored between 21 and 24. Now before you go patting me on the back, saying, "Well, done!" my finances scored a … 10. Yes, that's right – A FRICKIN' TEN.

I was not amused.

I was devastated.

I knew in the spring that I wasn't going to get another paycheck until mid-summer; so, why didn't I make a car payment? Other things took precedence. So, come the summer I made one car payment to stop the repossession; and although I was grateful to be able to do this, it wasn't … enough. I was facing the best working schedule of my life in the fall with good money, great benefits, and a sweet paycheck which allowed me to finally put in motion my divorce and really take care of myself well. Yet, still, it was not … enough.

So on this awakening Thursday, I broke down and borrowed $20 from a friend, who also chipped in another seven dollars for some ointment I had to help her back; I called my mother, and she confirmed she'd send the money. Through the meltdown, I realized that although I'd utilized all the opportunities G-d had sent my way, and although I lived frugally by most standards, it still wasn't enough.

As G-d planned, my car financing company called, and we agreed to see if I could renew my notes with them at a little higher interest and lower payments for an extended period of time. I contacted my apartment leasing agent to see if I could use my larger-than-necessary deposit to catch up on the rent and work out payments for these next two months.

Then I remembered the oddest letter I'd gotten from my insurance agent. I realized I hadn't shopped for car insurance for 13

January

years and quickly found out that I didn't have to pay $256 a month for insurance; I could, in fact, pay $90 a month for twice the coverage.

It was time for a change. If I was going to break the cycle, I had to do my thinking now, when there was no fear and no anger, but plenty of determination.

But, the changes were not just with the insurance. I went to my budget and starting putting my bills in order of how much they cost, not when they were due. I took a hard look at what I had and realized I could have all the same stuff but, I could get it for less or by changing what I had to include less.

Yes, I know the movie channels are only an extra $20 a month; but if I don't watch them, that's $240 a year that I'm wasting. And do I really NEED a second phone line for faxes when all I've been getting are junk faxes; or a second cell phone if all I'm getting are text messages from some creep I don't know? If I need to send a fax, I can just plug in my land line, do it, and save $10 a month. And for what do I need a second cell phone? Business? What's wrong with the cell phone I have?? It didn't take me long to hope that my renewal for my car went though and to realize if it did, I could give myself an extra $100 a month, pay off two personal loans for an additional $200 a month, put a bit in savings and still SAVE $710 a month. Just so you know … that's $8,520 a year!! I could buy a small car for that!!

And even though the savings was great, what was even better was that my paycheck could cover it all. Instead of driving myself nuts trying to make more money, I was actually, for the first time in my life, living within my means. Yet that was not all.

There was a freedom in knowing that for so very long I'd tried to pay off those two personal loans with the mindset that if/when I got the money to pay them in full I would. This translated into any extra dollars that came in would go for them. The problem was the extra money didn't come in as that is not what extra money was supposed to be for; extra money was supposed to go for something nice for me.

Tagging the extra to pay a bill or a debt owed meant there wouldn't BE any. Now, paying on them a little at a time would free up any/all extra money for the … extras. I sincerely believe by just changing this mode of thinking that there will now be extra money now that it is correctly designated.

Planning
    There is an odd comfort to be able to do this. Yes, there will be more rough roads ahead, as cycles do continue, but with a solid financial foundation, my mother believing in me, and G-d leading the way it's much easier to weather the storms.

C – Comfort

January

COMFORTABLE SHOES

Men are like shoes.

Really, they are.

I was cleaning my flat this morning – something I do only when I want to do something slightly more enjoyable than what I SHOULD be doing. Today, I tossed a pair of shoes into my living room closet. They promptly landed with the rest of my shoes in an untidy pile on the floor of said closet.

Seeing them sitting there instantly reminded me of my newest boyfriend; two thoughts that wouldn't normally go together—a pile of shoes and my guy—collided. The reasoning flashed me back to viewing his closet—a place in which all of his shoes were lined up neatly with a clean pair of matching socks stuffed into each pair. Now, I've not got a closet fetish. A shoe fetish is a different matter, but I remembered this because I'd not seen something like his closet before. And I would NEVER have suspected to see such a thing in a guy's apartment. Oh, I should probably mention that this was the norm in all FOUR closets in his house.

Realizing that I don't like being outdone, and I was still avoiding other work, I sat down to put my shoes in order. The least I could do was match them and make some use of the shoe stand sitting empty in the back of the closet.

Over the last year, I've dated 15 men; I currently own 22 pairs of shoes. Putting the shoes in order, I realized there was a connection between the two.

I had several pair of stiletto heels in different colors and several men who were great to go out to dinner or the theater with or even to work with.

I had several pair of stiletto ankle boots, and several men who were creative, spunky, and a great deal of fun.

Additionally, I had a couple of pair of sandals, and a couple of guys who were just a bit too in touch with their feminine side.

Then there were ankle boots with the chunky heels for the guys who looked good but were too overpowering.

Planning

Lastly there were the several pair of odd shoes bought for reasons I still don't understand and relate to the men I dated that I also still don't understand.

It was while doing this that I realized just how much men really were like shoes. They are functional when needed; they come in a variety of shapes, styles, and colors and they have a tendency to need to be broken-in before the fit (or non-fit) becomes apparent. On the down side, not every pair goes with what you are wearing at the moment; sometimes they either pinch, or are too big and fall off, and sometimes you don't know why, but there is just something about them that you don't like. They seemed like a good idea at the time, but turn out not to be.

So, as I'm sitting on the floor, staring into this now nice, neat, orderly, closet, I realize two things. One, I'm thinking of my current guy again, and two I'm holding the loafers I'd just chucked into the closet.

I only own one pair of loafers; they're brown. Fact is they are the only pair of brown shoes I own and match absolutely NOTHING else I own. They are ugly—they are probably the ugliest pair of shoes ever made. Everyone I know hates them but me.

I bought these shoes because the ones I was wearing at the time were killing my feet, and I still had a long day ahead of me. I bought them in brown because the store didn't have a pair in my size in black. I also spent an outrageous $82 on them because I had the money and really needed the shoes!

I also wear them every day as they are the most comfortable pair of shoes I have. I wear them when I want to feel good—when I'm sporting my blue jeans and my oversized oxford shirts. I wear them when I go to the grocer or the mailbox or downstairs to chat with the neighbor. No, they don't go with every thing I wear, but they are the first pair of shoes that I grab when I want to just be me.

I'm holding them as I find there is no more room on the stand; and the thought dominoes begin to fall.

Why is it, do you think, that we will wear a pair of shoes that no one likes but us, but we won't get serious with a man until he's faced and passed the "family posse"? Why do we need their opinion, permission, or input? What do they know that we don't, and why should we listen to them in the first place? Why is it, that when we dress up for the night, we grab the stilettos and find that we cut the night short because our feet hurt? Besides the fact that everyone else is wearing them, and they match our new dress, do we need this acceptance? Why do we expect the men of our life to fit with everything else we have, but we don't expect that from our shoes?

And most importantly, why do we let others dictate what's comfortable for us, when they've just as many shoes in their own closet?

All I know is that every time me and my guy have gotten together, I've worn my loafers. Lovingly, I look at these loafers. They're scuffed and stained, worn out in just the right places, comfortable and functional, and most of all, fill a need.

I set them on the floor, in the middle of my closet, right where they always are; confident that they will be there when I need them. I realize right then, that, no, my guy doesn't fill all of my needs. He's just there when I want him, comfortable in his own way, filling the need I have at the moment.

Quietly I close the closet door and smile. Yep, life is good when you're wearing comfortable shoes.

Planning
E – Environment

PRODUCTIVE OR BUSY?

I was very productive on Sunday; so I took Monday off.

I was incredibly productive on Tuesday; so I took Wednesday off.

But I didn't plan it that way. I didn't wake up Monday and Wednesday and say, "Well, I did so much yesterday, I won't do anything today." Fact was, Monday I was hoping to get a head start on my homework and then put out some really good e-mails, and after my super day on Tuesday, I'd planned to take all day Wednesday to do my homework up for the week.

But, it didn't work out that way.

My to-do list on Monday was simple: write, check the mail, do my budget, go to the bank, meet with a client, and take a meeting with Davis. Well, maybe it WAS more productive then I first thought. Wednesday was supposed to be an all-day study session. So, why didn't I hit the books? Why was my production limited to sending a renewal client a thank you note, filling out three to five job applications on line, and just lounging? Oh, and getting a quick tutorial from the cable guy on how to use the new DVR box.

I'd like to think that it was because I needed a day of relaxing, but I know better. There is one major problem with working out of your home: if the house is a mess, you don't get anything done. If there is clutter around you, it transfers to clutter in the brain.

And that's the problem. I realized this was a problem when I found myself apologizing to the cable guy because the room with the TV in it had piles of folded clothes all over. It's 11 p.m., I've not got my studies done but, it's time to get BUSY being productive, and the first step is putting up those clothes.

It's a little thing that weighs on our mind: the dishes that need to be done, the trash that needs to be collected and taken out, the clothes that now need to be in the closet. Even if it's not EXACTLY the way I want it, at least it will be done.

Then, I can become productive again.

January

SUMMARY

As you focused on GRACE this month, did you see a parallel to an issue in your own life? The following ten questions may help you gain new perspective on how to manage it.

Questions to ponder:

1. Is this issue bigger than me?

2. What is my part in resolving the issue?

3. Is now the right time?

4. What's stopping me?

5. How do I remove the barriers?

6. What resources will I need to get started?

7. What resources do I have?

Planning
Answers to Act on:

8. What isn't working?

9. What is working?

10. What's the next step?

To do List:

February

ACCEPTANCE

February is a month of acceptance. You've done a lot of hard work in the last months on your personal journey, and now it is time to take a deep breath to adopt the changes you've made. During this time of integration, focus on …

- **G** for GENUINE
- **R** for RECOVERY
- **A** for ACCEPTANCE
- **C** for COMMITTMENT
- **E** for ENTHUSIASM

Acceptance
G – Genuine

REBUILDING, AGAIN.

Sometimes we have to tear things down to re-build something better.

I'm doing that—again.

I'm not stupid, and I do listen. So, I got to wondering what it meant when three different people, who'd known me either for months, days, or minutes, all told me the same thing: Find yourself!

Each had said I needed to be honest with myself; and I was. I just wasn't honest with *them*. I took the good they had, saw the potential they had, and thought I could be good with anyone. I didn't tell them all the bad stuff they had.

Oh, sure they had their own baggage—their past wrongs, drug usage, alcohol abuse—and well, they weren't exactly the upstanding, honest, honorable people they portrayed themselves to be. I thought it was a small price to pay for all the good stuff we had. I was mistaken.

So, I find myself rebuilding—rebuilding myself, my image, my inner core—and the only way to do this is to tear down all the barriers I have about relationships and rebuild them.

There's nothing hidden with me; I don't shield people from who I really am and—I guess, in essence—from myself. Is it because I think I'm so wonderful that when they see me as an open book they will love me despite my flaws? Not really; it's simply because I haven't figured out how to slowly reveal myself a little at a time.

Why would I want to? Past experience shows me most people, especially me, don't know how to deal with a woman who doesn't play games—who says what's on her mind and answers with honesty. The mask has become the wall and, in essence, the "game." Is this "game" worth playing? Is the risk worth the reward? I don't think it is.

I remember moving from Michigan to Arkansas; it was quite a cultural shock. My brother asked me why in the world I would want to do this. Why would I want to sell everything that wouldn't fit into a semi-trailer, leave my business, my friends, my family members,

February

and everything I'd known for 20 years, to move into the backwater of society?

The answer was simple: to start over. I found that to go forward, I needed to get back to my core—to rip away all the things I'd collected that really weren't me and get back to who I really was.

I've done this several times. This time, it's different. I'm not giving up my home, my cars, or my personal possessions. I'm not giving up my community; I'm just re-evaluating—not giving up—my attitude.

I believe G-d sends us messages in threes; He tells us something three times in an effort to be heard. When we don't listen there are consequences. I feel I've been told to get back to my core, get back uptown and out of the gutter, become my authentic self, know myself and make others prove their worth instead of giving them the key to my heart. But, does this mean I have to wear a mask or put a wall around my heart? Does this mean I keep my mouth shut instead of speaking my mind? Does this mean I sugar-coat my responses instead of telling the truth with tact? No.

It means I get back to who I am: the writer, the teacher, the woman, the mother, the keeper of the faith. Maybe I'll be a bit more careful with whom I let in. Maybe, instead of putting up my mask to temper what I say until they are proven, I'll just step back a little—give them some room to either prove whether they are worthy or they aren't.

But then what do I do? I don't know. Maybe I'm not supposed to know. Maybe I'm just supposed to say, "Okay world, here I am!" If I am true to myself, then I'll be true to others; and that is all that is needed.

In an attempt to foster a relationship, I've let a lot of people into my inner circle, trusted many who were untrustworthy, only to find hurt when I did. However, the opposite of letting someone in, is keeping them out. How true to myself is it to keep people always at arm's length? How much of a personal connection can we make if I hide behind a wall just to protect my heart? It seems akin to being in a prison—a self-imposed prison at that! Isn't it better to give your all and fail than it is to give only what is necessary and win? I feel hiding behind walls and playing games is very much like lying to myself.

Acceptance

The struggle is in figuring how to be true to myself, without having a wall around me; not letting people all the way in until they prove they are worthy; and not getting so hurt that I don't try again.

That's a lot of rebuilding – or maybe, just maybe it's not. What if all I had to do was be myself, trust in the Almighty, and let the relationship unfold as it will? And if I do what I know is right, and then if the relationship ends, well, I'll keep the lessons, knowing I was true to me.

R – Recovery

February

GOOD BROKEN

I have a favorite coffee cup.

It's broken.

I refer to this as my Memphis Cup, mainly because I got it about nine or ten years ago on one of my many trips to Memphis. It's not an expensive, fancy, cup; it cost about a buck and a half. It's ceramic, has little bumps in the side where an air bubble or two tried to escape the glazing, and it's a very pretty powder blue. And, like I said, it's broken.

I can't remember when I chipped the lip of the cup.

I can't remember when my daughter-in-law dropped it and broke the handle off. I do remember that when she threw it away, I retrieved it from the trash bin. I don't recall if I found the handle parts, but I probably did; I do recall that I didn't fix it.

So why in the world, when I've a dozen or more other coffee cups, do I use this one when I need to feel comfort? Is it because, like the cup, I too have my chips, my bubbles where the clay wasn't just right, or am broken?

There are a lot of things I will and won't do—drinking coffee from a clear plastic hotel glass is one of them. So it was, on this trip, I found that I did not have a "real" coffee cup. My first night on this Memphis trip I found myself walking down Beale Street and came across a dry goods store. Making my way through the mishmash of their offerings, sitting tucked under a variety of other cups, I found this light blue one. Always being tight with a dollar, I found the price tag right, and the fit of the cup to my hand was a good one. There are some cups which are too big, and some that are too small; this one was a perfect fit.

That weekend did not turn out the way I'd planned. Through a scheduling snafu, I was left with a weekend to myself in Memphis to do as I pleased. I chose to write and wile away the hours being good to me.

So this morning, I found myself with too much time and too few things to do. I am in the midst of what I like to call "The Great Clean Up"—the one week a year when I clean up all the little things that I've been putting off. It's the time of year when I unpack some

Acceptance

more of the boxes I've had for years; clean out the filing cabinet; attack the two foot pile of mail; straighten the bathroom closet so I can open it and not have things fall out; and in general, take a hard look at the clutter in my flat and deal with it.

As is my custom, I needed coffee. I looked at the cups in the cupboard and chose my Memphis cup. Oddly, it occurred to me as I retrieved it from the cupboard how very much like people this cup was.

I had to be cautious when I used it so as not to cut myself on the remnants of the handle; equally as so, I needed to be certain I didn't drink from the chipped side. But, the cup still held coffee; the handle parts still gave me something to brace my fingers against when I used it; and the chip – well the chip was small when I looked at it from one side, and much larger when I looked at it from another, so I chose to look at it from the small side. This cup gives me a gentle reminder of a time when I was very good to myself; it fits so nicely in my hands, and it holds one of my most cherished pleasures.

I can't help but wonder, when we who see ourselves as chipped and broken and in need of being rescued from the trash bin, do we ever realize all the good we still hold inside? Do we see all the support we offer with our broken edges or all the comfort we can give by just being? We can give others gentle reminders of how good they are, how well we fit together, or how we may hold their most cherished pleasures.

I don't know. All I do know is that my Memphis Cup is perfect just the way it is, and I'm not going to try to fix it. I'm just going to allow it to give me the comfort I need. When we are broken, may we remember that this is what makes us fit so well with another.

A – Acceptance

February

LIBERATION

We think of boundaries as things to keep us contained.

But, sometimes, just sometimes they are what set us free.

I don't know why I called my mother, but I did. I was sitting at home, minding my own business, enjoying the leisurely Sunday afternoon, grading my students' final projects and final exams when the thought occurred to me ... call your mother. I brushed it off and said I'd do it later.

Both times; by the third time, I picked up the phone and was dialing her number before I had a chance to think.

As was her custom, she raved on and on about the things that made her feel important, and I gave her the support and kudos she was looking to find. Then it was my turn to do a bit of bragging about the "important" things in my life: finally getting my MBA, my acceptance into another college, and my conversion process at the end of the month. Not expecting her to make the trip for the conversion party, I told her it was okay that she didn't.

And then ... it happened, and something inside me snapped.

As was also her custom when I told her something remarkable, she discounted it by comparing it to something inconsequential. For example, when I mentioned that I was being considered for a Pulitzer Prize, she said that was nice and had she mentioned that my brother had just gotten out of an alcohol rehab center? When I mentioned I was on the wait list for a one-year fellowship at Harvard, she said that was nice, but did she mention that my sister had gotten a job as a janitor?

You get the idea.

So it was, when I mentioned my conversion, she said, "Oh, I don't think I'll make it as my boyfriend just had back surgery and ..." That's when I snapped.

"Stop, mother," I said in my calmest voice. "I'm tired of you discounting all of my important achievements by comparing them to some inconsequential happening in your life. I'm tired of you showing me just how very much other people mean in your life and how I am of no concern. I'm really tired of you showing me just how low a priority I am for you. And I'm not going to let you do it again."

She was speechless. But, as a fool who doesn't know when to shut their mouth, I continued. "I don't even know why I chose you as my mother. But, I will admit, I've learned a great deal from you."

She didn't understand what I had meant, and countered by saying, "I chose you because I wanted you, and I loved you."

The fool occupying my mind and controlling my mouth continued. "No, mother, you can stop with the lies now; you NEVER wanted me," I said with a sigh. Then I broke every level of social graces, every manner of British respect, and a commandment in the process, when I said, "And as for loving me, well, the way I see it, if you really loved me, you wouldn't have stood back and watched as someone—an adult—abused me."

There, it was out, the family's secret shame that we never spoke about. It was my turn to be shocked and appalled at my own words; at the fact that I would EVER speak to her in that manner.

Her voice cracked as she said, "Well, I guess my parenting skills aren't as good as I thought they were."

"No," I said, trying to regain some of my composure. "It's not a matter of skills. You did the best you could at the time with the tools you were given. But, I'm not going to stand for you discounting me anymore."

The rest of the conversation didn't mention the incident again; there were no defining moments left to come; there were no excuses as to why it happened or why she allowed it. I ended the conversation stating that when she wanted to have another adult conversation to give me a call. I wasn't hurtful, or mean, or even sarcastic as I'd been in the past. I was just quietly, firmly, setting my boundary.

I had a short talk with the Almighty when I hung up the phone. His words were ones of hope and joy at my actions, saying, "It's about time." I apologized for breaking the commandment of honoring my mother and father. His words were reassuring, "First they must be worthy."

I didn't know if I was giddy or terrified! Never had I treated my mother ... like an adult. She was always my ... mother. As her daughter, my role was clearly defined. It was my job to take care of her, even when I was too young to know how to take care of myself; it was understood that I would respect her, her wishes, and her things, though this was not returned in kind. She was not to be questioned; her actions were to be above reproach, and to do

February

otherwise was a manner of disrespect that I would have been punished for doing.

It was as if all along I were the adult, the caretaker; and she was ... the child, a willful child to be certain. She could come and go and do as she pleased; she was not to be questioned nor held accountable. Again, even as an adult, these were not luxuries I was afforded.

As I lay back on the parlor bed, my hands shaking, my face temporarily absent of tears, one thought blazed across my mind: I am ... free. No longer did I need to care about her, her opinion, her wants, needs or desires. She could fend for herself and could do so very nicely. She no longer colored my judgment, my decisions, or ... my life. This was not a bad thing in any language – it just took awhile to sink in. When it did, when the freedom to really come and go and do as I pleased became a reality, my whole life shifted. I recognized that I truly was only answerable to me and to G-d.

So, I guess it was upon waking this morning that an even greater sense of freedom surrounded me to the point where I started looking at relationships which had power—real or perceived—over me and made the decision to walk away from them: to do what was necessary to end them. No, it won't be easy, but rarely is change free from pain.

Acceptance
C – Commitment

ALONE

They tell me you must be good alone before you can be good with someone else.

They did not, however, say you had to like it.

That's where I find myself: alone, and not much liking it actually. I'm guessing it's because I'm trying to figure out where it is written that you must be committed to providing for the welfare of someone other than yourself to be socially acceptable.

Yet, I'm finding that I like be only committed to me. I'm not so sure it's a bad thing. Why is it when a man from my past called extending an invitation for a movie that I nearly said no? Perhaps it was because the emotions I once felt for him, the potential I once saw in us and the connection we once had, was gone.

He was a strikingly good looking man; he had a good job he held for the sole purpose of buying his dollhouse mansion in a community straight from a Hollywood movie set. He was a great kisser, and we fit comfortably. Our goals, however, couldn't have been more different. Where his life's ambition is to retire in seven years (at the ripe old age of 55) to spend the rest of his days "having fun," I've got bigger plans;—aspirations—dreams even. I have more commitments to myself that I want to fulfill.

So, I here I sit with my cat hiding under the bed in my very clean flat with the rent paid, and nothing to do and all kinds of time to do it. I wonder where my focus is.

Alone. The word doesn't strike fear in my heart, but it is an empty word that echoes in my head when it's late at night, all is quiet, and I whisper it to the walls. What is there to be good at when there is no one to talk to, share a meal with, or touch? How much easier can it be to get along with ourselves when we know we can go where we want to go, do what we want to do, and eat, drink, and be merry as we see fit? Is this really being committed only to us, a lifestyle with no room for another; is it incredibly selfish even?

The challenge comes in finding the right person to share these things, to find new things, to make each other better, and to do more than what we can do alone. Being alone, I'm finding, is easy. There's no one to answer to, no one to disappoint for not

February

doing something, no one to make a mess, or break something, or disagree with on some point.

The problem with being alone is that it is too easy. It's too easy to get so comfortable with your own life you don't have room for anyone else; too easy to realize it is much less hassle to stay in then go out; and much too easy to realize you don't NEED anyone to survive and live a good life.

The only really tough part about being alone is the motivation factor: staying motivated to clean the house, take care of ourselves, and concentrate on the employment matters; to fulfill the commitments we have to ourselves and for ourselves. After all, we are only accountable to ourselves and to The Almighty. There is no one to expect us to clean the house, take care of ourselves, or make a living; sometimes the discipline to do all of those things can be a bit trying.

Yes, living alone is easy; but there are times when I really miss the right person sharing a meal, talking about a bit of nothing, stealing the covers, and hearing the laugh at the private joke.

Maybe someday I will find that person—the one who looks good, has some social graces, is articulate, funny, and compassionate—the one who wants more out of life than what they have, and who can see the value in what I have to offer.

Until then, I will be very good alone, but I still have my doubts about liking it.

Acceptance
E – Enthusiasm

PLAY TIME

I've worked really hard this weekend.

So, who's got play time?

My to-do list for this unexpected four-day weekend changed as a revolving door. I made up a master list on Thursday, added and subtracted on Friday; but by Sunday there were so many things to change on it, I just went by the seat of my pants doing one thing, then another. Sometimes in life, as in school, we need a time out – a recess – a play time just to rejuvenate our souls.

It was a strange set of circumstances which led to the busy-bee flurry of events this weekend. I'd spent the better part of the last three months fitting the puzzle of my life together; but now, well, I needed to do a bit of catch-up; little things that had gotten pushed aside were now mounting. To add to the pile, I needed a change – something, ANYTHING, that would make my life different with the hopes that "different" would translate to "better."

I didn't know I could paint the walls in my apartment until I saw my neighbor do it. Over the course of the last two weekends, my living room is now two shades of khaki, my bathroom and one wall of my office is Fairy Lily Yellow ... but, I didn't stop there ... I also finally got around to sewing the curtains for my bedroom, hung my curtains in the living room differently, and added a coffee table. But, why stop there with the improvements? Hmm? On Thursday I graded all my students' papers, recorded the grades, and during the weekend found time to print out new attendance sheets, figure up class averages, do a two-page report with additional book recommendations for my meeting with the VP of Education on Tuesday, then did my own homework. Of course there were also the weekly chores of laundry, dishes, taking out the trash, vacuuming, cleaning the clutter (mainly the mail) out of my office, with the bonus being the ever wonderful task of cleaning up the mess of painting. Did I mention I also colored my hair and am planning on spending the day putting together a thirty-plus page draft of my research project?

As I look at my patio door, I am reminded of the bit of play time I was afforded. It was when I took down the trash, checked the

February

mail, and was bringing up some bottles of water from the car that I looked about me for the first time in a while. I noticed that the leaves, which had been brilliant shades of yellows, golds, reds, and oranges, were now starting to fall to the ground and turn brown. "Such a shame," I said to myself, "that I couldn't just bottle them up and keep them for the winter."

This in turn reminded me of when I was child starting elementary school. It never seemed to fail that the first craft assignment of the year was a fall-leaf mobile. You know the practice; take a bunch of leaves, put them between two sheets of waxed paper, iron them, then cut them out and hang them from strings attached to a wire coat hanger.

I didn't have a wire coat hanger; fact was, I didn't have any waxed paper either; but, I did have leaves. So, I set about taking a break from my work and collecting about twenty or so leaves. As I had to go to the grocer to get cat food anyway, I figured I could pick up some waxed paper as well. I knew my little ironing board was hanging on the back of the bathroom door, and I might be able to find my iron.

It was nice to stand in the kitchen with the little ironing board on the counter and the iron plugged into a socket I didn't even know was there under the high counter, arranging leaves on waxed paper. I made two big layouts of five or six leaves; then a couple of pairings, and two or three singles, and one of three. These were not going on hangers, so I could do with them as I pleased.

And what I was really pleased to do was to remember to take time to play. I didn't know where to put them when I'd finished ironing, so I just waited and went about my work. When I made my way back to my desk I realized I had a perfectly good, and empty, set of patio doors to which I could tape the leaves. And so I did. But, it wasn't enough of a reminder, not really. So I took one coupling of leaves and taped it to the other window – right above the eye-level of my laptop screen so as I look at the screen, in the background I can still see the leaves.

As I sit here this morning, I am surprised. I'd thought taping the leaves to the windows would just preserve their color and be a nice reminder to take time to play; what I didn't count on was what they would look like when the sun shone through them. As sun-catchers they become brighter somehow, their detail more pronounced, their design just ... more.

Acceptance

"Maybe," I thought to myself, "...maybe that is what happens when we take the time to play." As we go through our daily routines, dealing with the stuff of life, when we take a few moments to let the joys of play time shine through us, we, too, become...more. I've got my bottle of soap bubbles at the corner of my desk; my crayons and coloring book in my parlor, and now my leafy reminders to use them. May I remember that to fully become the adult I want to be, I need to remember the child I am.

February

SUMMARY

As you focused on GRACE this month, did you see a parallel to an issue in your own life? The following ten questions may help you gain new perspective on how to manage it.

Questions to ponder:

1. Is this issue bigger than me?

2. What is my part in resolving the issue?

3. Is now the right time?

4. What's stopping me?

5. How do I remove the barriers?

6. What resources will I need to get started?

7. What resources do I have?

Acceptance
Answers to Act on:

8. What isn't working?

9. What is working?

10. What's the next step?

To do List:

March

ACTION/ADVENTURE

March is a month of action and adventure. Your work has been mostly mental so far. However, now is the time when things are about to get exciting. It's time to set all your shiny new goals into motion. During this time of liberation, focus on …

G for GIFTS
R for REACTION
A for ALLEGIANCES
C for CONFUSION
E for EMBARK

Action/Adventure
G – Gifts

TEN DOLLARS WORTH OF MOTIVATION

I hate vacuuming my apartment.

Well, that's not really true.

I hate doing all housework—laundry, cooking, dishes, dusting, taking out the trash, uncluttering, you get the idea—but I REALLY HATE vacuuming my apartment.

It's gotten to the point that it takes me three days to do the job. The first day, I take the vacuum from the closet and set it in the middle of the living room floor. The second day, I plug it in. By the third day I'm so sick of seeing that stupid vacuum in the middle of the floor I turn it on and vacuum the whole place. Did I mention that this entire job can be completed in less than 30 minutes?

To completely clean my apartment takes less than an hour. The only thing worse than cleaning my apartment, is the thought of paying someone upwards of $50 to clean it for me. That's the problem with vacuuming—you have to do all the other stuff—dishes, trash, dusting, you know the list—BEFORE you can get to vacuuming.

So, here I am, hating to clean my house, hating even more paying someone else to clean it, and getting strange looks from my cat. Enter, Natalie. Now Natalie is a very good housekeeper, she has a gift for it; she gets paid very well to clean others' apartments, but, she's getting out of the housekeeping business and getting into selling insurance. I can see why she would.

But, she has one job left; it's on Wednesday afternoons. I know this because I watch her take the trash out for them, and then leave about 30 minutes later. I have an idea. I stand on my patio and yell down to her from the third floor. "Ya got 20 minutes to make a quick ten dollars?" I call down.

"Doing what?" she asks.

"Vacuuming my flat."

Her right eyebrow shoots up as she contemplates lugging her vacuum up three and a half flights of stairs. "Your vacuum broke?" she calls back up.

"Nope," I reply, "you can use it if you want." The deal just got sweeter for her.

~ 94 ~

March

"You want anything else while I'm there?" She's got her eyes on her watch now.

I look inside and go through the list in my head. "Nope," I said. "Just need a vacuum."

"For ten bucks?"

"Yep, that's the deal."

She thinks about it for a minute.

"Give me 20 minutes?" she asks.

"Got it!" I say.

YeHa! Nat's going to vacuum. What a gift to me! Now I need to clean before she gets here. As a Tasmanian devil, I hit the kitchen: put away the dishes, load the dishwasher again and start it, dump out the old food in the fridge, wipe everything down, and grab the trash bag. The trek through the house is done collecting trash as I go: one in the bathroom, one in the dressing room, one in the parlor, the kitty litter box while I'm there, and finally, the one in the office. As I go, I pick up the clutter. I pluck one of those pre-moistened dust cloths from the package and make the rounds dusting as I go. One more time with the cloth that does the windows and mirrors, and, woo hoo! The house is clean, and I've still got five minutes to spare.

I empty the vacuum into the now overflowing trash bag and tie it off. As she comes in to vacuum, I'm taking down the trash. Well, that's not exactly true either. I actually toss the bag of trash off the patio and then jog down three flights of stairs to pick it up and put it in the dumpster. To my credit, I always buy the good bags so they don't break and make a mess.

By the time I get back up, my office is vacuumed. She does that room first, and I can relax. I don't watch her vacuum, I feel it rude somehow. So, instead, I write.

"All done," she calls out. I pick up the ten dollars and take it to her as she's putting the vacuum back into the closet. "You know," she says as she takes the money and stuffs it in her pocket, "I don't know why you have me vacuum; your house is always so clean without it."

"Yeah," I say. I thank her again and think to myself, "Riiiiiight!" It's then I realize we all have gifts; special talents we can give to each other; gifts we can give which far outweigh how much they cost.

Action/Adventure
R – Reaction

DECISIONS

There's a light at the end of the tunnel.
And this is a *good* thing?
I'm not so sure any more. I used to think that ANY light at the end of the tunnel had to be better than floundering about in the darkness; could I be mistaken?

It is a natural presumption when one hears another say, "I see a light at the end of the tunnel," it is a good thing. The statement generally signifies the person's time of darkness and despair has ended and they see hope for things getting better. But, what if it's an oncoming train?

What if through all of the darkness what we see as a light of salvation is something which can possibly cause us more harm than what we are currently facing? In the same analogy, if we are presumably on the track in direct light of said train, what do we do about it?

Ahh, therein lies the challenge. Let us visualize for just a moment. There's you, in a tunnel, and a light in front of you. That's simple and usually it's clear enough to get a picture of the situation. It is *a* picture, yes, but maybe not the *whole* picture, or even the *right* picture. What if the tunnel was the Queens Borough Tunnel, with you and a hundred others racing through it at break-neck speeds? It's lit, you're in a car, and separately but together you and many others are traveling the same road. What if you're standing on the track of the El Train at McCormick Place Station in Chicago; but, there are more than one set of tracks? Or what if, it's just some little footbridge tunnel with a slow moving steam engine lazily making its way through the back country of some no account little town?

Yes, we do make some presumptions about us, the tunnel, and the train. And there is another one we make which is even more radical than those I've mentioned; that we have no choice in the matter.

What brought this all about was a recent conversation I had with my new-found friend; we were just chatting about this, that,

March

and the other, when she innocently said, "When are you going to stop letting the train decide?"

She put into clear focus how I am a reactionary; someone does something, I re-act to it. That's not always a bad thing; but like the on-coming train, I sometimes feel I have no choice in the matter. I let them do what they do, and I just deal with it as well as I can in the moment. The flip side to being a reactionary is when there is no one around to react to, I do nothing.

In a nut shell, we presume: there is a train, we are on the tracks, and it will run us over. Will it? There are many things in this situation I can't control, and nearly as many as I can. When we presume all the other things about us and tunnels and trains, aren't we also presuming if we do NOTHING the train will hit us? What if it doesn't? What if the tracks swerve before it gets to us? What if the train stops, derails, changes tracks, or a host of other things which we can not only *not* control, but that have *nothing* to do with us whatsoever?

If indeed we see the train has no other course than to run us over if we stay on the track, can't we just decide to step off? Could we not jump over the train? What if we did a two fold action of first stepping aside, then as it started to pass, jump on it, and go for a ride? Now that would be a trick!

And what if, just what if, WE became the engineers of the train? What if we stood firmly in the middle of the tracks; held out our hand at shoulder height; and said, "STOP!"? Add wonders to wonders, it not only stops right as it gets to our feet, but we slowly walk around and board the train – not as a passenger, or cargo – but as the engineer.

Yes, we can do all of those things but it takes one small detail to make it happen; we have act. First we have to decide that we WANT to do something to stop the light at the end of the tunnel from engulfing us. Then we have to take action to make it happen. We also have to realize at different times, we will be in different tunnels with different trains approaching. As such, our actions will be determined by what we decide is in our best interest. We need to move from the reactionary platform; from the helpless victim to the powerful engineer.

Sometimes we feel like we are in some Dudley Do-Right cartoon where we are the helpless damsel tied up by the evil villain to the train tracks with a speeding locomotive bearing down on us

Action/Adventure
waiting for the hero to do his job and save us from eminent harm. When all we really have to do is stand up, step off the tracks, and let the train pass us by. The decision is ours.

A – Allegiances

MULLIGAN'S

Draw a line in the sand, jump over it, and declare a Mulligan. But, what if it's a yellow line?

Starting over, or declaring a Mulligan (a golf term), is not new to my children or my grandchildren. It was common practice that when one was having a bad day, they would stop, draw a line, jump over it, and declare a Mulligan. It was a process for changing a bad day to a good day—wiping the slate clean and starting over.

When looking at my life and examining the relationships I have, I ask again, what if it's a yellow line. Yellow, as red is for stop and green is for go, is the international color for caution.

Yellow lines and their consequences are not new to me. I'm very familiar with the yellow lines on the El train platforms and the danger of crossing them and having a train nearly hit me. Yellow lines are also three feet away from the wall at the museum; and I know the humiliation from a good dressing down in front of my family from a security guard when I've crossed it. And these canary-colored lines also mark the "Prisoners Only" walkway in a state penitentiary, and I know the panic as I accidentally crossed one and had prisoners in my face showing me the error of my ways.

Yellow lines warn us to use caution.

So, why is it, do you think, that at this point in my life, where I am drawing lines in the sand, when I am starting various aspects of my life over, when I am determining the boundaries of all of my personal relationships, that I would even consider coloring some of those lines yellow?

And if some of those lines are yellow, could some of them not also be red or green? If I am going to cordon off the areas of caution, can I not also cordon off the areas of stop or go?

More importantly, shouldn't I?

What can I use as my guidelines to determine the people I no longer want or need in my life? And what do I use to determine those who can stay, but I need to be cautious around?

'Tis true no man is an island; but there are some people in our lives who are toxic at best and we need to learn how to love

Action/Adventure

them ... from a distance. We know these people are not safe for us; they have their ways about them that we just can't seem to get away from, and they suck us into the drama of their life. These are not good people for us. They hurt us, make us feel small, and have some measure of control over us in a variety of different ways. We need to color these relationships with red – danger – stay away.

There are also the really good people who are the best friends we've always wanted; they support us, give us comfort, and help us develop healthy, giving relationships. They get the green light.

Now, we're back to yellow; the cautious relationships we need to be aware of, distance ourselves from, give due-diligence to so as not to be hurt by them.

And maybe, just maybe, the possibility of getting hurt is the guideline I need to use to determine who these people are and where they fall in my life. Add to this, can they be trusted? What is a friendship when the person hurts you or can't be trusted? Well, I think it is a toxic relationship; one that I don't need in my life.

Get out the crayons; I'm going to be drawing a lot of lines; and in the process defining my life.

C – Confusion

March

CONFUSION

I didn't feel like writing today.

Fact is, I don't feel like doing much of anything at all.

Seems this state of standing still is beginning to fuel a state of confusion, disappointment, delusion and discomfort; it really makes me wonder what the difference is between this state and the state I was in last September when no aspect of my life worked.

For all of the growth I've seen in myself, my relationships, and my life; I'm just wondering – when does the joy of where you are going, overcome the pain in getting there? I want to take comfort in where I am – the employment opportunities that are on the rise; the bills being taken care of; the relationship with my family members being in a good place; and most importantly, my relationship with the Almighty being better than it ever has been before.

But I can't help but feel that there is still something missing.

As I examine how I really feel, I realize there are A LOT of things missing: fear, anxiety, chaos, and stress come readily to mind. There's an old Chinese parable about a man who goes to see a wise man. The wise man asks him if he'd like a cup of tea. The man says yes, and as he's making himself comfortable, the wise man begins to fill his cup. He does not, however, stop when the cup is full; he continues until the cup is overflowing. "Stop! Stop!" cries the man. "My cup is overflowing."

The wise man smiles and says, "Ahh, but you see; your cup IS overflowing. You must first empty it, before I can fill it up."

We go through life filling up our cup with experiences to the point where we are overflowing; then when we want to embrace new ideals or (as in my case) a new life; we must first get rid of everything we have in our cup to make room for the new stuff.

I'm beginning to realize this standing still level has an emptiness to it I'd not expected. As leaning backward brought a familiar pain with it; standing still brings an emptiness; and the hope is, that stepping forward will bring a joy. Of course the grand hope is that the joy of stepping forward will overcome the pain of the leaning backwards; but, will it? I don't know.

Action/Adventure

What I do know is that right now, my vessel is empty; I feel hollow inside. It's not so much a bad thing, as it is a new thing. What do I do when I feel empty inside? Do I just go through the motions doing the things I know I need to do to get me to where I believe the Almighty wants me to be? Do I rejoice in the little, everyday blessings which lay all about me? Is the Almighty giving me little glimpses, little hopes, that my relationships are on the right track? That my career is going in the direction, He wants it to; and that I am becoming all that He hoped I would?

I'd like to think so.

Everyone tells me that the Almighty always answers prayers, and I believe this. However, I don't believe His answers are always yes or no; I think sometimes His answer is, "Not right now." There's a hollow feeling when the answer is "Not right now." It means that we need to work on what needs to be worked on. We need to rejoice in the little blessings. We need to have faith that we are on the right track, and we need to wait.

March

E – Embark

A TIME TO DO

Thinking is a very good thing.

Yet, there's something to be said for doing as well.

I've held tightly to my dream of teaching throughout the school year, and then going to Europe or South America for the summer since I had the dream back in 1985. At the time, I wasn't qualified to actually teach and was just starting a business and for some reason thought the business would afford me the ability, resources, and freedom to take the summers off. I was mistaken.

But, I didn't let go of the dream.

So why is it, do you think, that even though I had this dream I was stunned, shocked even, when the opportunity to make it happen presented itself?

It was last Friday when I started thinking about what I wanted to do for my birthday in June, and I'm always getting these e-mails that say "Visit London." I had just gotten one for the holiday specials. Just for fun, I went to their website and found for ONLY $6,800 I could spend two weeks – with air fare – in four star accommodations around the time of my birthday. I chuckled at the price tag, but I also said out loud, "Okay Almighty, if that's what you want for me, show me how to make the money to do it."

This was not unusual for me as I've often based major decisions on my ability or inability to raise the money. If the money comes through, I do it; if it doesn't, I don't. It's pretty simple really.

So I find myself smiling at the prospects and go on about my way. By Saturday night I'm telling a good friend of mine about the possible trip, and I casually mention that it's too bad I couldn't just get a summer job in England so I'd be able to take weekend jaunts to Paris, or maybe even Israel; and wouldn't that just be WONDERFUL!

Bam!

It was at that moment I felt the two-by-four of awakening between the eyes. Why COULDN'T I find a job in England for the summer? My current job at university wouldn't suffer if I took time off or better yet, only accepted teaching on-line classes. I could raise the money necessary to carry me over the summer from now until then; and all I'd need is someone to watch my cat.

Now, the question is, are there any openings? A quick internet search turned up over 150 colleges and universities in the UK; I sent my favorite university a quick e-mail saying I'd like to teach there for the summer and asked how do I do this?

By Monday, this same university was opening the door of possibilities. This dream was quickly becoming real; not certain, but, the doors were opening.

As I worked on doing all that I needed to do to forward this dream, two sad thoughts occurred to me. The first was the history with my ex-husband, or as I used to call him, "The NO Man." With each opportunity I'd dream up, his first response was "NO," and it would be a fight with him to take advantage of it. Never mind that he rarely had to actually DO anything to make it happen; all he had to do was accept or give permission for me to do it. I felt it was sad that I had to ask permission to live my life as I saw it. It surprised him when I got tired of asking permission and resorted to just TELLING him I was going to do things. He didn't care for that much either, but, at least I kept my dignity and took advantage of the opportunity as well.

The second thought was, just how very much like him my ex-boyfriend was. Although he never actually SAID no; he was always one to want to keep all of his options open to the point of while he was waiting for something that he thought was possibly better to come along or while taking his time thinking about whether he wanted to commit to the opportunity, he missed the opportunity that was presented to him. Time and again, opportunities for him to enjoy something would present themselves, and while he was waiting for something better, or trying to make up his mind, the opportunity would pass by him.

He couldn't commit to a barbecue with my family, so he sat at home. He couldn't accept dinner at my place, so he ate alone. He couldn't pick up the phone to call me, so he stayed in silence. He couldn't accept all that I had to offer him … so he lost me. I've often wondered if the sanctuary of his home wasn't, in fact, his prison. Although he believed it to be his respite from the world, keeping the bad things at bay, could it not also be said that it also prevented him from enjoying all the good things the world had to offer?

March

There's something to be said for safety and solitude; quite another to be the gatekeeper of your own prison.

There are some who sit and wait for good things to come to them; there are some who only think and dream of good things happening; there are some who go out and seek good things to take advantage of; there are even some who come up with good things and work towards making them happen. Then, well, then there are some who just sit, and wait, and think too long about the good things they want – and they lose them.

I don't know if I'll end up teaching in England; but I do know that if I do nothing but sit, and think, and dream, the opportunity will be lost. There is a time to think and a time to do; may I always realize when it is time to stop doing one, and start doing the other.

SUMMARY

As you focused on GRACE this month, did you see a parallel to an issue in your own life? The following ten questions may help you gain new perspective on how to manage it.

Questions to ponder:

1. Is this issue bigger than me?

2. What is my part in resolving the issue?

3. Is now the right time?

4. What's stopping me?

5. How do I remove the barriers?

6. What resources will I need to get started?

7. What resources do I have?

Answers to Act on:

8. What isn't working?

9. What is working?

10. What's the next step?

To do List:

Action/Adventure

April

GROWTH

April is a month of growth. With all the changes you've made and the new habits you're forming, you should expect a time of tremendous evolution. During this time of development, focus on …

G   for GROWTH
R   for RENEWAL
A   for ADAPTATION
C   for CONFIDENCE
E   for ENGAGE

THE SPOILED CHILD

It is rarely attractive to watch a spoiled child beg their parents for something.

It's even less attractive when you realize you're the child.

So it was that I found myself this morning driving back from the veterinarian's clinic when I started again my daily prayers.

Of course I was grateful for all of the good things that were going on in my life: the renewed university contract with additional classes, a pay raise, and a bonus; the additional classes before my Judaism course were finished; the three weeks left before my MBA final class is finished and that I'm actually doing well this time; and there's the fact that with just a bit of squeezing my rent will be paid close to on time with a renewed lease with no rent increase awaiting my signature. As the cherry on top, there was the very real possibility of teaching in the UK for the summer.

Yes, I have a great deal to be grateful for in my life. I should have stopped there. I should have just said amen and turned to something else. But, as is my custom, I didn't; I pushed one step too far; I once again asked for my heart's desire--my miracle.

In that instant, I was reminded of the time when my children were young. My habit then was ask once; if the answer was yes, they got it; no, they didn't; maybe, they better not ask again. My own words came back to haunt me. "You will get it, if and when, I decide you need it."

Ouch.

Was it not me who in my child-like antics was going to the Almighty, asking again and again, whining, crying, and throwing my own version of a temper tantrum to get what I thought I needed and what He had denied me for His own reasons? I could almost hear Him sigh and say, "Enough already! What? You don't think I heard you the first thirty times? You think crying and whining and asking again and again is going to get it faster if at all? I'm working on it; let that be enough."

I was ashamed. Upon my realization, I did the only thing I could think of: I apologized. "I'm sorry," I whispered, tears streaming down my face. "I'll not ask again." I paused. Well, that

April

wasn't really something I could stand behind. "Unless," I added, "I'm in a moment of weakness."

I find myself in a place where what I want is not available. The longing I have is, at times, overwhelming. But, each time I get just a taste of it, I want more. I realize that it is not because I'm greedy; it's because the little I get isn't...enough.

I'm old enough to know that if a little is good, that does not necessarily mean a lot is better. However, I wonder if the area between *too little* and *too much* isn't *enough*. As in the tale of "The Three Bears," Goldilocks found that one was too hard, another too soft, and the third just right. Maybe I'm looking for my place of just right.

I'd like to believe that I am not a greedy, spoiled child. I would like to believe my needs are satiable--that I neither ask for too much nor give too little. I would also like to believe my faith in the Almighty is strong and steadfast.

Yet, if I believe all of that, I must also believe I am human; I am a child. There are times of darkness when I need my Father to comfort me; I need Him to understand that my whinings are not those of a spoiled child but a begging for understanding, and that my tears are not a ploy to get my own way, but an expression of my pain.

There were many times when I didn't give my children what they wanted. Sometimes it was because I knew what they wanted would not be good for them and sometimes, just sometimes, it was because I had something better in store for them. I should always remember that when I don't get what I want, it is possible there is something better in store.

Growth
R – Renewal

A GOOD CRY

I don't cry over much.

Though I am sure there are those who would disagree with me.

Sure there's the heart-tugging commercial, the sappy chick flick, the unexpected kind gesture, but other than those things, what's to cry about? Oh, wait; I forgot physical and emotional pain. What was I thinking?

So it came as a surprise to me how some people just make me weep – openly even. Though I don't cry in front of them, I do find myself crying rather often on the phone when they break out in song; when they say they love me to death; and even when they said they don't want to continue the relationship. Yeah, I was a weeping willow; what's your point?

It was through this incredibly brief, but emotional, relationship I remembered something; just how to-the-soul good it feels to cry. The mere act of letting the tears flow drains you of toxins in your system; it empties your cup to make room to fill it up with the good stuff.

Crying reminds me of rain — the way the rain washes the dust from everything; the way the air smells fresh once more; the comforting feeling to know that all is new again. I've always had a fascination with the rain, with thunder and lightening storms. Some may say it relates to the day I was born when it's reported that three tornadoes hit the town where I was born. My grandmother was always quick to add, "No, no. I believe there were four." It may be because on the days my sons were born, it stormed; although one was born in October, the other in April; and both in Michigan. It could also be that it rained a solid downpour for four straight days before my son's wedding, only breaking at noon on his wedding day. When the storms come, and they do come fast and hard, I sit in the living room and watch them; it's a comfort somehow.

I told a friend about my 100 days of tears. There was a point in my life when I was so downtrodden, that I cried for 100 straight days. After hearing my tail, my friend agreed that after 30 plus years of sorrow, it just may take that long for all the toxins, to be

April

purged. It was then I realized it was only through the love of family that I stopped the tears and began living my life again.

Life is pretty darn good and a nice hard cry is good for the soul. Please pass the tissue.

Growth
A – Adaptation

TEACHERS

He is a very good teacher.

I am all the better for it.

They tell me when the student is ready, the teacher will appear. I think they are right; I guess I just didn't understand the lesson that I was to be learning. Generally speaking my best lessons are the kind given with a two–by–four right between the eyes. So it was with some surprise and trepidation that this lesson came to me quietly, with kindness.

It was no secret that deciding to have dinner with a married man was quite the struggle for me; that it turned out to exceed my wildest dreams was a wonderful bonus.

Yeah, sure, we all see the movies where the man is attentive, and pulls out the chair, and is nice to the waiter, and has charming conversational skills, and even better conflict resolution abilities for their own control issues. But, what happens when they materialize right before our eyes? What do we do then?

What do we do when we find someone who actually listens to us? Who really cares about knowing what our needs are and then tries to fulfill them? Do we trust their words or their actions? And to top off the surprises, what do we do when their actions ACTUALLY follow their words?

In my case, I count myself very, very … lucky. And then, well, I learn from him.

It wasn't so much what he said; but what he did, especially what he did when I didn't ask him. For example, he picked me up a gift that I'd forgotten I'd mentioned I liked. He also opened the car door, let me walk in front of him, introduced me to the waiter, called the waiter by name, tipped him very well, and got MY car for us so I wouldn't have to walk in the rain. These are all very little things; yet, things I'd not been privy to with others.

It was also what he didn't do, as in he didn't get mad when we got lost – several times!! He didn't get nasty when my order wasn't right – twice – and he didn't start eating until I got my food done right. He didn't yell at the manager to get them to fix our bill; but he did have a difficult time accepting when they did.

April

It was strange to hear a man say he was sorry, when he was wrong; and stranger still when he didn't chastise me when I was. His first answer to any problem was to laugh about it, then figure it out, and he could get very serious about it in the process.

This was all so very new to me that I did the one thing I do so very rarely; I was myself. I didn't put on airs, or try to show how smart I was – better still – didn't act stupid to stroke his ego. He is one of the few people who've ever seen the real me straight out of the gate.

I guess the overlying factor that surprised me the most was – I REALLY LIKED IT. I liked not having to pretend to be interested in something I wasn't; I liked asking for what I really wanted and getting it; I liked not having to act like an idiot to make him feel smart; and most of all, I liked the way he took care of me without asking, without being told, without expecting something I wasn't willing to give.

Now, if I could just find all of these qualities in a significant other life really would be grand.

Maybe some day I will find someone who can meet my needs, who will care what they are and will care enough to try. Right now, however, I've learned I am worthy of that person; that my needs and wants are important and I deserve … better; I deserve to have them be important, deserve to have them met, and deserve to have someone who will listen to what they are.

Yes, he is a very good teacher; and I am so much better for it.

Growth
C – Confidence

DRESSED FOR SUCCESS

I bought a bathrobe today.

It's short and 100% cotton with a little hood on it.

It's reversible: blue on one side and blue and white stripped on the other side, all trimmed in purple. I didn't realize that they were my favorite colors until much later after I'd bought it.

As I sat, cutting my nails, as I had broken one waaay too short to be able to type well, I started thinking about how my interest in writing has again been sparked. And I realized that there are certain clothes in my life that spark that interest—oddly enough—they are bathrobes.

My first bathrobe was a gift, and my writing was stilted, harsh, without as much feeling as it should have. My second robe was a big, white terry cloth number that I got with the UPC symbols from my cigarettes, and because I gave it to myself and I had earned it, my writing became more whole, more complete, and more rounded. I still have the robe, and when I'm in need of inspiration, I wear it.

The next bathrobe was handed down to me from my grandmother as I was the largest woman in our family besides her who could actually wear it. This is the one I wear when I need comfort or my writing needs focus.

This brings me to the one I bought today. I'm trying to change again—to be more stable, to wig out less, to be in a position to add some spice to my life without making it all consuming. I'm trying to get more into the travel writing market and this robe is just a bit funky, fun, comforting, and more like the me I'm trying to become.

If our clothes make us who we are, then this should work; if they don't, then I'm just the strange woman on the third floor who meets the UPS guy in her pajamas and bathrobe. But then again, we don't usually dress for others; our clothes can easily be an expression of how we are feeling, the task at hand, or the mask we wear. What if we wear what we do to make us feel like we want to feel? What if I sport my bathrobes in an effort to put me in the mindset I want to be in—not the one I AM in?

I think that's the way it works, and I'm so very good with it.

E – Engage

MISS ALICE

I don't want to become Miss Alice.

It frightens me to think I just may.

A week ago today, my neighbor Miss Alice moved. Just like that. No notice, no nothing; not even a good bye. I saw the moving van pull up and before noon, she was gone.

Granted, she did just move to another apartment inside the complex, but it was strange to see something so very "permanent" suddenly be ... gone.

Miss Alice was a daily factor in my life; if I thought my TV volume was disturbing her, I'd turn it down. If I had a gentleman caller, I made sure they were quiet coming up the stairs. Or if I had some flowers delivered I was allergic to, I'd offer them to her first. I'd even make her cookies for holiday time and hang then on her door knob.

I can't say she and I were friends; we were neighbors; we were good neighbors in the sense she lived her life and I lived mine, and when our paths crossed, we'd chat. I'd never been inside her apartment, and to the best of my knowledge, she'd only been in mine once. It was then she discovered she liked the layout of my apartment better than her two-story town house and decided to get one for herself.

Miss Alice has always been my neighbor; she was the only constant neighbor I'd had. For three years, we shared a wall between our bedrooms, and I could tell when she was upset as she'd slam her dresser drawer shut, and it would rattle the pictures on my wall.

I didn't know her well; she worked for the city police department, had about five more years until retirement, was about that many years older than I am, was hiding out from an abusive ex-husband; and to the best of my knowledge never had a single friend stop by for as long as I've been here.

She's a nice looking woman; friendly when we'd meet on the street or in the garage; smart, too. But, her routine was nearly set in stone: she went to work at the same time every day, came home at the same time, and stayed home until she left again the next morning. It was as if you could mark her comings and goings with a stop watch; the only variance was the every other Saturday when she did her grocery shopping.

She didn't go out at night, to dinner with friends or a gentleman caller; she didn't have people over on the weekends or any other time; she never attended any of the gatherings down at the complex's club house; and besides her job, I don't know of anything else she did. Except for two people, once her niece and the other her brother, and the apartment maintenance crew doing work, I'd never seen a single person go to her door.

Of course, over the years I'd invite her over for dinner or a BBQ; but although she'd accept, it never happened. She didn't go to services on Sunday; or have pizza delivered; or even have packages which needed to be signed for. The only reason I even knew her name was because I got a letter for her in my mailbox by error; and it was only because I recognized the address on the envelope that I even knew it was for her.

Many days when she left for work, I'd watch her walk from the stairs to the garage and there was always this air of ... sadness about her. It wasn't depression, but I never saw her smile unless she was looking directly at you. She was quick to laugh during conversations; but, you had to make the first move ... always.

I don't want to be like her. I don't want to live my life in my hovel, removing myself from human interaction, and spending so much time ... alone. I know I am good company, but I also know all of my favorite jokes, would like more than one opinion on something, and just think it's fun to be with another.

It's Friday; a cloudy day to be sure. My plans are simple enough. First, finish the chores I didn't get to yesterday—putting away the clean dishes, folding and putting away the laundry, mopping the tiles—then attending services tonight. It's also Memorial Day weekend and although I've no major plans for Monday, I do have an appointment with my massage therapist Saturday afternoon and dinner plans for Saturday night, possibly attending services on Sunday morning, and lounging by the pool Sunday afternoon.

It's not a lot; it's not a jammed pack schedule of back-to-back events; but, it is something. It is getting out into the world and seeing what's going on about me; it is interacting with others; and it is far better than starting down the trail to isolation. I guess what

April

scares me the most about Miss Alice is that I understand her. I am painfully aware of just how very easy it is to hide from the world; to take comfort and solace in living alone and not having to try to get along with another; to not have to continue the search for the right person to share your life with; and to have the desire to search be beaten out of you.

I've been where she is; not for a long time, just bouts of isolation here and there. I don't like it at all. What I don't like about it is that I feel like I'm not doing my best; I'm not giving anything to any one; like I'm hording all of my goodness for no other reason than I'm too afraid of getting hurt to take a chance on letting someone in.

I never want to be that afraid.

Growth

SUMMARY

As you focused on GRACE this month, did you see a parallel to an issue in your own life? The following ten questions may help you gain new perspective on how to manage it.

Questions to ponder:

1. Is this issue bigger than me?

2. What is my part in resolving the issue?

3. Is now the right time?

4. What's stopping me?

5. How do I remove the barriers?

6. What resources will I need to get started?

7. What resources do I have?

April

Answers to Act on:

8. What isn't working?

9. What is working?

10. What's the next step?

To do List:

Growth

May

COURAGE

May is a month of courage. At this point on your journey, you will need boldness and strength to continue down the path. Don't lose heart! During this time of bravery, focus on …

G   for GOODBYE
R   for REVOLUTION
A   for AUTONOMY
C   for COURAGE
E   for ENDURANCE

THE SILENCE

A period goes at the end of a sentence to show the thought is finished.

So what goes at the end of a relationship to mark its completion?

"Good bye" is always good. "I never want to see or hear from you again," or "Yes, that is a restraining order," are also good ways.

I habitually find myself driven to have the last word; there is always one more thing I feel the need to say, one more point I feel important to make, only to be met with silence.

I realize in life it is not always what you say, but how you say it. I also recognize it is incredibly rude to meet someone's words with silence; yet, maybe it is this silence—the lack of words, the lack of communication—which is screaming the relationship has ended.

The men I've known knew the one thing I couldn't stand was to be ignored. They used this knowledge often, and it started a cycle in which they would say something, I'd react, they'd met this reaction with silence, time would pass, and the cycle would start again.

Yes, there was always a level of expectation that I would forgive their bad manners, and all would be right with us again. But, when I didn't, and they weren't, any attempt of them believing this would be delusional. It's funny how I always wanted the chance to give them back their own silence—do to them what they were doing to me, rather like giving them their own medicine and seeing how they liked it, and thinking that if given the opportunity to see how much it hurt to be ignored, they would stop this behavior.

I was never able to follow through. I don't know if it was my own arrogance in believing my words were important, or if I just can't be that rude. Maybe it was a matter that I felt the tidbits they gave me were the beginnings of something real. I don't like believing the worst of people, especially men I cared for. I don't like believing those I have known were more interested in playing the game than they were in building something real. I realize now, my silence wouldn't hurt them, and even if it did, it would be short-lived.

May

    Maybe I just felt the need to say something, anything, to get a reaction from them, and believed their reaction confirmed that we had some personal connection. To add to this line of illogic, I believed if they reacted, they cared, and if they cared, we had something. The truth is there truly is a time to say goodbye to relationships that are toxic in nature or just plain not good for us.

    There is a time when saying goodbye is a healthy choice for us. Up until now, however, I'd always let them have this choice and not given it to myself. I'm realizing this was not the good thing it appeared to be and saying goodbye was not a bad thing at all; even if my "Goodbye" is equally as silent.

WISHFUL THINKING

Finding the right partner is like putting together a puzzle.

So, why can't we mix and match the pieces?

If I had a magic wand, I'd make my own partner; I'd take the good pieces from each of them; and create my own puzzle.

But, I don't have a magic wand; so it is just wishful thinking on my part to believe this man is really out there? Or has the purpose of the men I've known been just to show me what I really want? Has this journey just been an adventure of discovery or has it really been to search and find the right partner?

What if it's none of the above? What if it wasn't about them at all? What if it was all about me? Could it be the good I saw in them, was actually my good reflected back to me, and the bad I saw in them my own bad behavior magnified in the return to show me what I need to change?

I feel another two-by-four between the eyes coming.

If I made a list of all the issues the Almighty was trying to show me I needed to change, the list of issues would look like this: all the evil baggage, all the fear, uncertainty, and inability to make decisions, and the hidden lower-than-acceptable social class and attitudes.

Well, now, that's quite a tidy little list, now isn't it? Could the handwriting be any clearer on the wall? I don't think so; well, maybe if it was in neon lights, but that's just presentation.

So, now, what do I do?

Last night my Rabbi told a tale of a man who sent his son out into the world to learn a trade. The son discovered he loved to make chandeliers; so he took it upon himself to study under the greatest chandelier makers of the time. Upon his return home, he told his father not only had he learned from the best, but, he himself had become the best chandelier maker in all of the land.

His father's disbelief was understandable, so the son showed him the chandelier he had made and to prove his point, he requested his father to invite all of the masters to come and view his chandelier.

May

An invite was sent throughout the land inviting all the masters to come, and they did. One by one they viewed the son's "masterpiece," and each in turn said the same thing. "That is a horrible chandelier! It has no form, no beauty, it is worthless...except for this one little part over here; and that is perfection!"

When all had viewed the chandelier, and each had confirmed what the father thought, pointing out one imperfection after another, he told his son he was a failure! He had not become the BEST chandelier maker, but had, in opinion, become the WORST chandelier maker.

His son laughed, and explained to his father, that his creation was one in fact comprised of all of the imperfections each of the masters' had; and it was in those imperfections that each of the masters saw their own perfection.

Perhaps the answer lies in the word imperfection. We are not perfect; we are human. Sometimes our beauty lies in our imperfections. So I have to ask myself, "Does the list of behaviors add to my beauty, my charm, or my value? Or does it detract from those imperfections which really do?"

I've tried looking at others and using their good and their bad as a guide to my own behavior. I find I am looking at their imperfections and choosing to adapt those that make me better and changing those that don't.

In my search to find someone to share my life with, the Almighty is giving me a list of things I need to change about myself. Perhaps it wasn't *my* wishful thinking of finding the perfect mate, but *His* wishful thinking that if He showed me what He wanted, I would become what He'd always hoped I would: the best I can be, imperfect in all. Where I have the ability to see the imperfection in others, He sees the perfection in me. This can't be a bad thing in any language.

A – Autonomy

ABANDONMENT

"Abandon all hope ye who enter here."

Words, it is said, which are written above the gates of Hades.

But, what about here on earth; does the same apply? It's not the hope part I question; it is the abandon part. What hope do we abandoned here? Conversely, is our hope gone when WE are abandoned?

That hit me like a rock between the eyes.

For the last few days one word has been swirling around in the back of my mind: abandonment. I'm not really sure what caused the word to be there in the first place; it doesn't feel like it was a divine signal or a healing phrase; it feels more like the accumulation of experiences and this was the logical deduction of their sum.

The question which boiled up from the mire of this sludge was: Do I have abandonment issues? In order to find an answer, I had to know what abandonment issues are.

As is my custom, I hit the internet to do some research. Terms I'd never been exposed to jump out at me: Outer child, abandonoholism, abandoner, abandonoholism. It took me only but a moment to realize something profound; it was if someone was holding a mirror to my face and saying, "See, this is you."

I could see myself in the list of situations in which "abandonment" occurred. I didn't know if this should be a concern for me, how big of a problem it was, nor what to do about it. I took a few minutes to think about the situations which caused me to feel abandoned.

I realized I do have abandonment issues. I need to face these fears. I want to develop my outer child to one who exhibits acceptable behavior; I want to love my inner child so she may flourish. I want to live in the world of my inner child, guided by my adult mother; to do so, I must let go.

I must let go of all of the sick, twisted, horrible, and horrific relationships of the past. I must welcome all new relationships with the joy of my inner child, be ever watchful of the acting out of my outer child, and trust all who I meet a little at a time. I must start each relationship fresh, new, without expectations, fears, and sins

May

from past relationships. I must go into the relationship with my arms and my heart wide open and be cautious until they prove their deeds do follow their words. And if they don't, I must be brave enough to walk away with the knowledge the failings which caused the ending are not mine, and be aware it was the other person's bad behavior which was unacceptable to me, not a reflection of my own inadequacy.

I am not excusing myself from acting badly and then putting all the blame on another; I am taking responsibility for my actions, and as such encouraging myself to only give my best, and to realize I am human.

In the same sense, I am holding myself harmless from all the people who took advantage of my kindness, who abandoned me for their own reasons, and I am apologizing to myself for my own actions which may or may not have contributed to the situations.

I am also making myself a promise: to recognize when my outer child is acting badly, to allow my adult mother to be her best, to allow my inner child the freedom to love, live, express joy and sadness, and to allow myself the pure pleasure of giving my all to another without the poison of the past.

"Abandon all hope ye who enter here." Perhaps hope is lost when we are abandoned, when others do not see the gifts we have, when pain is incurred, or when we don't get the nurturing we need as a child, and we let that pain and fear incubate as we become adults. Maybe, just maybe, it is not *our* hope that is abandoned, but *theirs*.

Maybe it is *their* lives which are the lesser for not knowing *us*, our gifts, and that which we have to offer them. Perhaps their act of abandoning us didn't just hurt us but also hurt them more because of it. And maybe, it is their hope that diminishes because of it. We who feel abandonment feel we are unworthy of the love and gifts from those who did the abandoning, yet it is really them who are the ones unworthy.

If they were worthy of our gifts they would have taken them, treasured them, and rejoiced in the receiving of them. But, they didn't. They threw away the treasure; they took only what they could see; they used only what they saw of value; then they blamed us for their actions; their short-sightedness wouldn't allow them to get the full value of what we have, what we are.

And maybe, that is good for us. For if they didn't take all that we have to offer them, that leaves more for those who are worthy to enjoy.

Yes, the pain of feeling unworthy is great; however, the realization that I was trying to give my gifts to the wrong people, and the hope of finding ones who are worthy, are greater. My inner child is rejoicing through the tears; the outer child is silently sitting in the corner sucking her thumb; the adult mother is gently gathering us both in her arms. She knows keeping these two in balance is going to be a challenge, but tears of joy stream her face as she realizes they are both here, together at last, in this place filled with love, and support, and hope.

C – Courage   *May*

FEAR

There's something to be said for fear.

It can save a life or destroy one.

In this case, it destroyed something wonderful, and there was nothing I could do to stop it. It's oftentimes been said of me that I am courageous, brave, and strong; that isn't true. What I am is incredibly selfish.

Now, selfish has had a bad rap over the years, and most think of selfish in the "spoiled brat" sense; some might argue I fit that description as well. Yet, there is another not so well known method of looking at the term, "devoted to or caring only for oneself" which colors my world.

When faced with a situation where my selfishness comes into play, I ask myself, "Am I so busy that I can't help a little old lady out of her car?" Of course not, so I take two minutes out of my day and help her. "Am I so important that I can't put $5 in the box to help those less fortunate than I?" Of course not, so I put in $10. Or more importantly, "Am I the type of woman who will only accept a man on certain conditions?" No, so, I loved him unconditionally, and it scared the daylights out of him; so we both lost.

Fear is a strange duck. He believed that, "Fear comes when one of us feels the other has expectations that we can't meet." But, I believe it can come from our own expectations as well as other's expectations. Fear can come from inside as well as from outside; it can be sudden or a slow burn; it can be a reaction to what is happening or based on our thoughts of what might happen. Yet, regardless of all of those conditions, once realized, it can be overcome.

It's not easy to live with fear; it's easier to face it if you know how. As I see it, facing fear means making a decision. The question becomes, "Is it easier to live with this fear or to face it head on?" Is it easier to be afraid that someone will realize all of our faults and that we are not the wonderful person they think we are, or to show them our faults one at a time and let them decide?

Ahh, therein lies the base of the situation. Whose decision is it? If we see our own faults, and we find them unacceptable, we believe others will do the same; hence, they will decide that we are unworthy.

The problem is: what if they don't? What if what we feel are our weaknesses, they see as our strengths? What if what we see are our past wrongs and failings they see as that which made us stronger? And what if, just what if, we see all of who we are and compare it to who we think they are, and realize that we aren't good enough for them while they think we are everything they'd hoped to find?

Whose decision is it?

If we take it upon ourselves to decide our worthiness for someone else, we also risk being wrong and missing out on something that could just be everything we hoped beyond hope to find. If we act with courage and we allow others to decide for themselves, yes we do take the risk of not being as worthy as they think we are, but we also allow them the freedom to enjoy all the good that they see which is hidden or covered up in our view of ourselves.

There's an old saying, "Be careful what you wish for, you just might get it." I did; I just wish he would have let me make my own decision instead of deciding for me. He was wrong.

E – Endurance *May*

G-D'S TIMING

I saw G-d's hand at every turn.

So, how come it still turned out badly?

Therein lies the crux of my confusion, doubt, and—if I'm honest with myself—fear. Rarely in my life do I do anything without the guidance or blessing of the Almighty, and maybe I've just lead a sheltered or blessed life, but I find when making the tough or major decisions that doing so with His guidance and/or blessing means that it will turn out good.

Not so much lately.

Fact is, although there have been blessings, gifts, and wonderful things galore, there are still a few areas which aren't turning out so ... good; and, these areas are starting to really concern me.

The first area of concern is my son's car. I had really struggled to keep up on the car payments, found myself refinancing the car, and just when I thought I had it all in order and things were going smoothly, he totaled the car—without insurance. To add insult to injury, the secondary insurance wouldn't cover it either. This does not negate the loan with a balance of nearly $19,000; no, this means that I'm still responsible for the note AND he doesn't have a car. So, I find myself with a couple of payment options on the note and one of them is to come up with 10% down and make affordable payments over the next few years. This lends itself to the dilemma of actually having the money in savings to do this; but, if I do it, then I may be cut short for the lean summer months.

I remember when I got the car for him; it wasn't his decision, it was mine. It was ME who thought it better for him to transport his wife and children in a safe vehicle. Maybe it was a decision I shouldn't have made. If I sit and think of all the woulda/shoulda/couldas I'd realize that I made what I thought was the best decision at the time, and things could have turned out much differently and cost more than just money. I also saw the hand of G-d in this decision; it was He who allowed the car loan to go through in the first place; it was no minor miracle that I got this loan two weeks after I got the loan for my own car.

Courage

    The second area of concern I have is my job. It was the hand of G-d who sent me to this university at the time when they needed someone with my skills, talents, and abilities. I love my job, but, as of late, the changes that are out of my control give way to the option of me not having this job come next term.

    The third area of concern is my education. The ease of getting into this school and the degree program itself was again, guided. So, why am I failing? I would like to think that it's all me, but, I don't think it is. Last weekend I'd planned to take all day Saturday and catch up my homework; my son came to visit unexpectedly. My priorities changed.

    I hadn't seen him since the accident in December, and it was a very welcomed visit. So, why did I spend the time when he left on Saturday doing my grades and then Sunday getting everything else in order?? I don't know. But, this week is Spring Break, and I'm looking forward to finally getting it all under control as much as I can.

    So, I'm back to the beginning; what do you do when you see that it's the right thing to do and it still turns out badly??

    I don't know; but I'd like to believe that they didn't turn out badly, that this was the best of the possible outcomes, and that the other options were even worse. I'd like to believe that for three and a half years, my son had a car that was safe to drive, that the changes on my job will be good for me, and that it wasn't time to work on my education and it is now.

    And maybe that really is the answer: to believe the Almighty has our backs even when we don't know it, to believe the bad stuff really isn't all that bad, and to believe we do have the best we can have for now. I'd like to believe it is faith and hope and knowing all is well which will get me through these changes.

    And maybe this is result in following the Almighty's guidance in the first place; to go places and do things which challenge us, make us better people; and maybe in the end, make the world a better place in the process.

    I can only hope and remember, when all you have left is you and G-d, it is enough.

SUMMARY

As you focused on GRACE this month, did you see a parallel to an issue in your own life? The following ten questions may help you gain new perspective on how to manage it.

Questions to ponder:

1. Is this issue bigger than me?

2. What is my part in resolving the issue?

3. Is now the right time?

4. What's stopping me?

5. How do I remove the barriers?

6. What resources will I need to get started?

7. What resources do I have?

Courage
Answers to Act on:

8. What isn't working?

9. What is working?

10. What's the next step?

To do List:

June

JOY

June is a month of joy. It is time to celebrate—to find joy in any hour. During this time of elation, focus on …

- **G** for GOODNESS
- **R** for REST
- **A** for ASPIRATION
- **C** for COMPASSION
- **E** for EXTRAORDINARY

Joy
G – Goodness

WORTHY

I am not worthy of receiving love from the men I've dated.

So, how can I be worthy to receive the love of the Almighty?

Struggling to find my own self-worth after falling from grace has brought me to this place; it is not a bad place; the sun is shining after several days of rain and storms; and it mirrors my own discoveries.

To better get a handle on where I am, I again attended the monthly healing service at Temple yesterday morning. I hadn't planned on crying; I never do; but the Rabbi's words cut to my very soul and were so astonishing to me, that the tears came without warning.

I had the honor of helping the Rabbi unveil the Torah; had the grace to give blessings for the miracles in my life for the last month; yet, found myself so astonished by her words, that as the tears streamed my face, and my whole body shook with emotions, I called out, "What did you say?".

To which she replied, "To know that to sit quietly and just be, is good enough."

How is it possible, my mind screamed, that to be worthy of the love and grace of G-d, one only need to sit quietly and just be; to be a faithful and obedient servant is the only thing asked of us; and to realize there is no shame in not being as wonderful, powerful, and all encompassing as the Almighty?

My perception of worth just shattered. I had been fighting for months to obtain love from the men I've dated and had failed. I realized this was just one of many battles I had been fighting and losing; the longest running battle was to attain the love and the accepted "worthiness" from my parents. If I couldn't win those battles, what hope did I have of winning the love and grace of the Almighty? Her words, however, put those battles into perspective by making me suddenly realize that there is nothing I have to do to EARN the love and grace of the Almighty; to realize that it is His grace and mercy which gives me this gift for just being. I realized I didn't OWE the world anything for being born – I was good enough by just being.

June

Again, I ask, how could this be possible?

If I consider the relationship between the Almighty and I as one of a Father and child; and I compare the relationship to the one between MY parents and I, it is not good. My parents made their displeasure of who I am and what I did very well known throughout my life time; they were never one to hold back with the harsh words, the strap, or the threats of being thrown away. They were, however, ones to not see the value in physical displays of affection, support of ones ideals, providing security, or big on giving comfort. It was not a relationship of us against the world; it was me against them AND the world.

There was not a time when I recall being "worthy" of their love and affection. I can't recall a time when my pseudo step-father hugged me or told me he loved me without sexual connotations; or my mother had anything positive to say about who I am or the things I've done; her remarks were not heartfelt when she did offer up the morsels or acceptance and normally were discounted by another's menial accomplishments which in her eyes bested mine. I don't recall a person (except my grandfather) in my life showing me positive reinforcement for the accomplishments I achieved; I do, however, recall countless incidents in which I was made to feel shameful, not worthy, not somehow good enough, for them to love me. How could I not believe that the Almighty felt the same way?

Looking back now, it seems that I was pretty much left to fend for myself from an early age; always engaged in some battle to win their positive support; failing this, and left to my own devices, I settled for the negative attention believing *some* attention was better than *none*, no matter how dangerous it was to do so.

Maybe this was the gift that they gave me; the lessons they taught me; the pain they inflicted; to make me the parent I have become.

If I change the parental example from the Almighty and my parents; to the Almighty and ME as a parent; the difference is remarkable.

I asked myself this morning, "What do my boys have to do for me to love them?" The answer was simple: nothing. Giving birth to them was a contract of sorts; with the life I gave them, came the love and all the gifts I had to offer as well. I remember when I first found out I was pregnant and my husband asked me what I was going to do about it, whether I was going to keep the child or not, there was no decision. I remember thinking; I will finally have someone to love me for who I am, no matter what. I did not realize that in the Almighty, I already had this.

If I carry the example of the Almighty and I as parents a step further, I also need to ask, "What can my boys do so I will *stop* loving them?" Oddly enough, the answer is the same: nothing.

There is nothing my children can do that will make me stop loving them. Yes, there are times when I just want to throttle them for their stupid acts; yes, there are times when I am disappointed in them for I know they can do better; and yes, the decisions they make for their lives are not the ones that I would make for them. But, it is THEIR lives, not mine. I have to realize the Almighty has given them the same freewill he has given me; and as such, I, too, need to realize that, no matter how much I WANT to, I CAN'T control their lives. They have to be free to make their own mistakes; knowing that I am here for them as I always have been; I am available to help, to give them my gifts, to listen, to give the advice I know.

But, that's where the example ends; because unlike the Almighty, my resources are finite, my gifts are limited, my knowledge restricted by my experiences, education, and resources.

Throughout my life I've believed that the relationship between the Almighty and I is reflective of the relationship I had with my parents. Additionally, in making this comparison I believed the love, affections, and worthiness my parents gave me, was also reflective as what I was entitled to from the Almighty. However, what if I changed this perception to mirror the relationship I have with my own children; to know that as I love my children unconditionally, He loves me as well? What if the reason for me to become the parent I am was to learn the kind of parent He is? I feel uncomfortable saying this; I don't know why. Perhaps it is because I don't feel worthy of making such a comparison; put in context however, it is the *relationship* I'm comparing not the grandeur of the Almighty to the grain-of-sand me.

If the Almighty truly is the type of parent I am; or the other way around; then He would accept me as I am; believe that I was born "worthy" of His love and all the gifts He has to offer; He would rejoice in my successes, be saddened in my stumblings; supportive in my endeavors; and expect nothing less of me than my very best.

Hmm. Seems to me, He already does.

R – Rest

June

REST

And on the seventh day, G-d rested.

I think it's time I did the same thing.

I've often said all I wanted was a day with no worries; so, couldn't it be said that a day of rest would qualify?

Normally, I can tell what kind of night I've had by the condition of my bed when I wake. This morning, it was apparent that the position I went to sleep in was the same as the position I woke up in; the bed was barely touched, and my earache could testify to what happens when you sleep for nine straight hours without moving. It was the perfect ending to the perfect birthday.

My birthday amazements (I'm tempted to say miracles) actually started just before one a.m. I'd not yet gone to bed for the day, but what I had done was taken an unexpected 90 minute "power nap" in mid-afternoon. I normally take 20-minute power naps between seven and eight p.m.; this day however, I found myself laying on the sofa, reading a book, and at about four p.m. slipping into the nap. I awoke 90 minutes later wondering why, but I was good with it.

So as I said, the miracles began just before one a.m. when my youngest son called; he teases he called was to ask me a question, but then wishes me a happy birthday thinking it would surprise me. What would have been the surprise was if he HADN'T called? He doesn't need to know that I'm onto his tricks.

We chatted for a few minutes, and I begin to get tired, so I readied for bed. About 1:30 I slipped into bed, suddenly wide awake. My thoughts started to swarm about how tonight, now this morning, is the only night this whole year in which there is a blue moon. I started thinking it would be a really cool thing to have a picture of it. So, I got up, grabbed my digital camera, and headed out to the patio to snap off a couple of shots.

I am amazed at what a clear shot I have of the moon and the few stars about it. The shots are good, but they are not really what I'm trying to capture. I realize my good camera is down in the car. By that time it was two a.m., and I was wondering if it's a good thing to go get it. I decided that it was. So I jumped into a tank top, jeans, and loafers and quietly made my way to retrieve it. I turned a couple of lights on when I got back to the flat, put all the equipment on my desk, loaded the film into the camera, chose the telephoto lens, and realized what a perfect night it was to get this shot.

Back on the patio, I'm smiling at the right framing I got when I noticed a car pulling into the parking lot. Judging by the time of night, and where the car was parked, I guessed it was my downstairs neighbor, the police officer who worked strange hours. I glanced around the tree to see a man that I didn't readily recognize get out of the car. I watch him for a minute and realize that my neighbor isn't as big as this guy, nor does he have this much hair! However, from the third floor, in the dark, I couldn't say as I know who he is.

I snap off another couple of shots of the celestial phenomena, and kept watching the man. I suddenly realized he was coming across the parking lot toward my stairs, and I tried to figure out which neighbor he could be coming to see. When he reached the bottom of the stairs, my world froze. It's my ex boyfriend.

When he got directly below my patio, I quietly called out his name.

He stopped and looked up at me. "Yes."

"What are you doing here?"

"Answering an e-mail in person," he replied. I didn't know what he was talking about. "Is it okay that I'm here?"

It took me about ten nanoseconds to reply. "Sure, come on up; I'll unlock the door for you."

So I did. I unlocked the door and went back out to the patio and continued. He came up behind me, stood in the patio doorway, and told me I picked a perfect night for taking photos.

So began the most perfect night we ever had together. No man could orchestrate the evening we had. Throughout the morning, he told me that it had taken him a long time to accept coming over to my house—to accept that which was behind my door. I was surprised. I felt as though he had accepted me.

I felt that our relationship is in a state of rest. You can't always go ninety miles an hour with your hair on fire; you will crash and burn if you try it.

After he left, I went about my day doing the dishes, the laundry, coloring my hair, and being in a state of wonderment. I thought it was very sweet of my ex-husband to send me a note

June

wishing me a happy birthday. I got a wonderful call from my grandson wishing me a happy birthday and was amazed when my grand daughter could actually SAY happy birthday! I received two dozen roses from their parents and shared many a laugh with my son when I called to thank him for the roses.

I went to my annual OB/Gyn appointment in the afternoon. My youngest son called again with warm wishes, but I'm here to tell you, there are few times in a mother's life when talking to her youngest son ISN'T a good thing: talking to him while flat on her back, naked from the waist down, during an OB/Gyn exam is one of them! I called him back.

Then I went shopping at the GOOD stores—a place where even if I HAD the money, I wouldn't pay THEIR prices. But, any time you can find two silk tops, marked at $78 each, and you can buy the pair for $20 total, I highly recommend doing so.

My daughter-in-law called on her way home from work, and we had a wonderful catch up conversation, and it was yet another of my blessings of the day.

Temple service that evening was one of celebration; a birthday blessing, a healing prayer, and filled with new friends and laughter. I said another prayer of healing for my friends and felt really good about it.

There was a mighty storm brewing outside when services began and broke just before the service ended; it regained with a fury after I was safely home.

The storm didn't frighten me; I'm not sure why, but maybe it has something to do with having been born on a day when three tornadoes hit the town where I was born. Storms bring me an odd sense of comfort. I love to watch them, find comfort in the rain, and though sometimes the loud noise of the thunder startles me, it doesn't really frighten me. It almost feels like during the storm is the only time I can feel completely surrounded by the Almighty.

My mother had called while I was at Temple, and I was surprised that she did. Surprised not in that it was unusual for her to call, just that she had done it despite us getting into a tiff a few days earlier.

So it is that this morning I awake, rested. I feed the cat, start the coffee brewing, make the bed, and check the emails from the night before. I realize that each of my relationships is in a state of rest; they are all in good places and will be until such time as something happens to upset those apple carts.

A time of rest brings us an unusual opportunity. We can take this time and revisit each of those situations in our lives which are at rest and choose what we do next. We have the option of going though and picking apart all of the things that DIDN'T happen, like none of my three best friends in the world calling me to wish me a happy day, or we can relax and ENJOY all of the good things that did happen.

It would be easy for me to worry and fret about the NEXT time I see Blender Man … or if I don't. It would be easy for me to call my friends and nag about WHY they didn't call me or to pout about it. It would be easier still to chastise my youngest son for his mismanagement of time and resources so I didn't get his present on the day.

But, I'd like to think that on His day of rest, the Almighty grabbed a cup of coffee, kicked his feet up, leaned back, surveyed all that He had created, and said to no one in particular, "Yep, life IS good."

We can choose to worry about what DIDN'T happen; we can choose to fret about what MIGHT happen; or we can choose to realize that right now, what is happening, is all good.

There is something to be said about resting; I'd like to believe it is a time to just stop, look about ourselves at our lives, and realize that life really is good right now.

A – Aspiration

June

NEW DREAMS

What do you do when your dreams come true?
You make new ones.

That may sound trite, but what are the other options? You can stay where you are; that's boring. You can try to recover the dreams you lost, but you lost them for a reason and some things need to stay lost. Or…you can make new ones.

The problem with making new dreams is that you have to start with where you are, not where you want to be, and go from there. When you are making new dreams, you take stock of what you have—what you like, what you don't like so much—and see what you may be lacking and where you want to be. It also means you have to leave some very good things behind because they are not yours to take with you.

The good thing with making new dreams is that it is forward movement with your life; it is moving upward and onward, and it can be a very exciting—if not terrifying—new journey.

There comes a point where you've met all the adult goals you've set for yourself to define the lifestyle you want to live; you sign the lease on the flat for the next year; you put money in savings; you finish up the settlement agreement on your divorce; you make the insurance premiums; you pay up the health, dental, and life insurance policies; you've started cleaning up your credit report, paying back the money you've borrowed and have enough to give a helping hand to others.

You realize you look about you and your flat is just the way you want it; your car is showroom perfect; you've got some wonderful new clothes; your weight is acceptable, and you have finally got a hair cut and color that you love. You look fabulous; your things are fabulous, and life, in general, is fabulous.

How do I make new dreams? I'm doing everything I want to do; I'm loving my job; I have all the material goods that I want; within the next two weeks, I will have put all the finishing touches on my life. I still need to get my front tooth fixed and some new glasses or perhaps contacts even. At that point, I will, in effect, become the perfect me. Now, that doesn't mean I'm PERFECT; it just means that I'm the best me that I can be.

Where can I take this new me? Therein lays a good question. What do I still want to do that I haven't done? Most of the "life dreams" I've had deal with large money matters. So, what comes with the making of these dreams? The big fear is that I will do things that will make my life so full I won't have room for another, that I'll not desire another, and in fact, will believe another will only mess up what I've done as opposed to enhancing what I've yet to do.

I guess if it were only up to me, and not the Almighty, I would have something to worry about. But, it's not just up to me. The Almighty knows what's in store for me; He knows the plan. He knows my heart's desire.

Dreams are what they are: wonderings of the heart, goals to shoot for, opportunities for G-d to make our lives better than we could ever imagine. So, I guess the biggest dream of all is that I will be ready to enjoy all the wonderful surprises He has in store for me.

C – Challenges

June

STUMBLINGS

I watched my youngest granddaughter fall on her bottom.

I must admit, she bounced rather nicely.

At fourteen months, she was one to go hell bent for leather until she tripped, stumbled, or for some other reason stopped and then fell back on her bottom. I thought it was because she was so joyful at having finally become vertical and able to move about of her own volition; I could be wrong.

She sat for a moment, looked me straight in the eye, and smiled. Apparently she had done this enough times to know what was going to ensue; it was new to me. Mere nanoseconds had passed when her older sister began with the cajoling to get her to stand; when that didn't work, she began pulling on her hands, trying to get her to her feet.

Not succeeding, her brother began his spiel to get her back on her feet. His was a bit more physical and ended by picking her up, to which she lifted her feet so he was still not accomplishing his mission. He sat her down, and the two siblings started fussing as to what to do.

About this time, Dad comes in the room and settles the whole mess with, "Enough already! Leave her alone!" The two older siblings sulked off in different directions; Dad looked on to make sure the youngest was still fine, and when all the commotion has settled down, She got back on her feet and was off–hell bent for leather once again.

I wondered at this turn of events as it may apply to adults and our lives. How many times have we stumbled and fallen only to have friends and family members come to our aid, unasked, and had the Almighty step in and tell them "Enough already! Leave her alone!" And when we get good and ready, we get back up on our feet and are off for another adventure as the Almighty looks on and smiles.

I'm not saying we don't need help from time to time as, Lord knows I've needed my share. But, what if the Almighty knew, I mean KNEW, that whatever came our way we could handle it and normally on our own? What if we all had the confidence of this little girl—that we KNEW when we were ready, we could get up off our bottoms and go again?

Would that be brave, or courageous, or maybe just living by faith? If we have the faith in ourselves we were born with, the faith that existed before the world beat it out of us that we could feel everyday, wouldn't that just be a grand way to live? How do we get that back?

I don't know; as I watched her squabble with her siblings (and holding her own rather well, I must admit) I wonder … how do I get back the gift that she lives every day? How do I trade the fear and uncertainty I have for what she has? I think the answer comes in just living every day, every moment, not as if it were my last, but as if there is forever, and in knowing somewhere, Dad is looking out for our best interest, no matter who tries to interfere.

E – Extraordinary   June

A MATTER OF CLASS?

We live in a class-less society.
Don't we?
And so it goes that I was sitting here tonight, watching an old rerun of one of my favorite television shows and the topic of the show was dating outside of your "social class"; and it hits me like a ton of bricks.

Rich bitch; snooty broad; living above your station; being too big for your britches; whore ... all the words that my mother, my family, and my ex-husband had called me; and in doing so ... making me feel ... unworthy; unworthy of my success, unworthy of my stature, and unworthy of ... the good life; and fearful I would lose it because I really WASN'T worthy of having it.

Through it all, I have arrived in my own fashion ... I live in an upscale neighborhood; with a tastefully decorated flat; a very nice new car; and a closet full of clothes for nearly every occasion. Then comes all the men in my life who have the social graces of a pig and each of them, in their own way, were unworthy of me, yet, made me feel ... unworthy of them and the life I've created. I see their potential only because I see it in me. I see the dressing down to meet with others status quo; I see the deep personal problems; I see the past of addictions ... and I know that deep down inside they are more than they appear ... because I am.

But, I am wrong ... they aren't, they aren't at all what I see -- they are what they are. I loved them for what I saw in them, what I wanted to bring out in me, and ... to quiet the voices of my past that made me feel unworthy. It was as if by dating someone below my own social class that I wasn't bringing them UP to my level, but was going DOWN to theirs, and in doing so suddenly became more humble, more worthy of my own success. It was like I was balancing some stupid scale -- my success balanced with their non-success -- hence I could now enjoy all that I have. This was the penance I felt I needed to pay to be worthy of it. This was the price I felt I needed to pay to live the extraordinary life I have.

Yet, I have been robbing myself -- as if throwing pearls at swine made the pearls more valuable, when in reality it just made them ... dirty. I think it's high time to wash the pearls, gently, in warm soapy water, scented lightly, pat them dry, and allow only those who can appreciate them to see them and enjoy them for what they are; a very unique creation of the Almighty, of beauty, of worth, of priceless value -- to the right one.

Of all the lessons I've had to learn, this was the one that made sense of all the rest. There really is nothing seriously wrong with me; no major flaw in need of repair; no past act so horrible that it will take a lifetime of penance to forgive; it was just a matter (as my son had so adamantly stated and as the Almighty has been trying to teach me) of me getting back up where I belong; of being the extraordinary person I am, and realizing I really am worthy of all of the good in my life.

I don't need to justify my lifestyle; change it to meet the demands of others; apologize for it because others don't have it; nor feel guilty for it because others didn't make the same choices that I did to get it. What I need to do is enjoy it; make it better; share it with one who is equally as extraordinary. And until such time as I find one who is worthy of sharing it, realize that *I* am worthy of having it all to *myself*. ☺

SUMMARY

As you focused on GRACE this month, did you see a parallel to an issue in your own life? The following ten questions may help you gain new perspective on how to manage it.

Questions to ponder:

1. Is this issue bigger than me?

2. What is my part in resolving the issue?

3. Is now the right time?

4. What's stopping me?

5. How do I remove the barriers?

6. What resources will I need to get started?

7. What resources do I have?

Joy
Answers to Act on:

8. What isn't working?

9. What is working?

10. What's the next step?

To do List:

July

EXCELLENCE

July is a month of excellence. You have much to celebrate! During this time of brilliance, focus on …

G   for GRAVY
R   for RIGHTEOUS
A   for ANTICIPATION
C   for CONTENTMENT
E   for EXCELLENCE

Excellence
G – Gravy

ACCIDENTAL LESSON

I didn't mean to hit him.

It certainly wasn't something on my to-do list!

I will admit, I am not always the sharpest knife in the draw; and sometimes it takes a while for me to understand the lesson the Almighty is trying to teach me; but, when I get it, it's like a two-by-four between the eyes.

Insert one oak two-by-four

As I sit here this morning, waiting for my neighbor to ready for work so she can follow me to the body shop, I got to thinking about the accident I had on Saturday; hence the reason for going to the body shop this morning! I was angry about the accident, and not for the obvious reason of HAVING the accident.

I was angry because the guy I hit wouldn't talk to me; in fact, he did everything he could to avoid me or ignore me. Every step of the way he did everything to shut me out; he wouldn't tell me if he was hurt; wouldn't take medical attention; resisted my request to see where he was injured; and throughout the police report portion ran away from me ... and the officer.

Where the officer was giving me comfort and aid, he had to hunt the other guy down to get the information or give him the paperwork.

As I sat here this morning, reviewing those happenings, I happened to mention to myself, "and he's different from any other man I've known?"

BAM!! The two-by-four did its job.

Frame by frame, or as much of it as I could remember that is, the accident played out in my mind; however, it wasn't my car hitting his car. It was me entering the lives of the men I've known.

Without warning, I hit them. There they were, going on about their lives, and suddenly there I was. They didn't expect me to ask them if they were okay, if they needed help, and they certainly didn't expect me to help them. But I tried; I knocked on their windows; I asked them if they needed an ambulance; I asked if they needed a doctor; I even made them show me where they were hurt. I followed where they lead and offered my assistance at every

July

opportunity. I tried to make right what I had broken; unfortunately, I didn't break them and didn't realize that it wasn't up to me to fix them.

Through it all, they ran away from me. They ignored me. They took what they needed as lightly as if I were trading insurance information. At the earliest possible moment, they left and didn't look back.

When all was said and done ... it was me who paid the final bill; the deductible, the rental car insurance, and the other short-term expenses for me and for them. But, it didn't stop there, for the accident would stay on my record for three years and the increase in premiums was an expense that I could ill afford.

Now, at this point I could be very jaded and angry both for the accident and for the men in my life; but, I'm not. Before you think me absolutely insane, the reason is two-fold. The first is that the headlight I was considering fixing from my last fender bender with a pickup truck would now be fixed. AND the dent in the tailgate that I get angry at every time I see it (which is every time I get into or leave my car) will also finally be fixed.

The bonus is, people were nice to me; the officer, the insurance guy, the claims' adjuster, the woman at the body shop, and the man at the rental car agency. I guess a final cherry on top was since I made two car payments payday before last, I could take the money I was going to put on the payments and put it on fixing the car.

It's odd in that all of this accident business my car will be looking show-room perfect when it's all finished.

And so will I be; I will be the perfect me when I finally finish the lessons I need to learn. I will be ready for whatever or whoever comes my way. I think it's a fair trade.

Excellence
R – Righteous

QUIET

Sometimes the quiet is deafening.
Other times it is a comfort.
Right now, as I sit here, the only two sounds I hear are the road traffic and the clicking of my nails on the keyboard. For all the complaining I do about being alone, I am grateful for the quiet.

I had been putting off talking to my mom about moving to an assisted living apartment for as long as I could; there was no more time, I refused to spend any more money, and I had exhausted all of the medical options to prove her doctor wrong.

The time was now. It was the right thing to do.
However, NO ONE said I had to like it.

Her visit to my home this weekend provided the opportunity for us to talk quietly. I've been told that I am the strong one in the family; I'd like to believe that. Yet, there is no amount of strength that can prepare you or hold you when your mother is as close to tears as you've ever seen her. There is no amount of strength that will keep your heart from breaking when she deems her work was for naught and that there is something bad coming around the bend. She whispers, "Then what have I been doing all of this hard work for?? What's next??" There is no amount of strength that will stop the tears when she says, "I'll show them! I'll work even harder and get even better! Then I'll go back home!!" And you have to say, "No, mama, you will never go back to your old place to live."

I was grateful that she was at my home—my quiet place for the weekend. I broke the news to her on Friday; we discussed it a little on Saturday; and then got into the nitty-gritty details on Sunday. I watched her deal with the pain, hurt, and confusion.

I explained everything more than once; I even detailed the medical explanations of WHY she could never live on her own again. I spoke to her quietly with love, kindness, and compassion. It scared us both a little when she took a tissue from her pocket and wiped my tears and made me blow my nose. She chuckled at the gesture, remarking on how very long it had been since she'd done it.

July

What hurts the most is I still don't think she understands. There is an underlying false hope about her; she is determined to show them (as I tried) that she CAN live on her own. She did not understand the futility of her hope. She can't see her own deficits, and I can. She can't see how long it takes her to dress, ready to leave, or take the stairs; she just sees that she CAN dress, ready to leave and take the stairs. She doesn't see when she no longer has control over her hand how she could hurt herself; she just sees that she doesn't drop her coffee cup anymore. She doesn't hear how she double-talks and forgets in mid-sentence what she was saying; I hear it very clearly. She doesn't see that moving is the right thing to do while I know it is the only right option.

She refuses to understand that her life will never be the same again; all she can see is that I'm the one changing it.

I sometimes wish I didn't have to do this; I wish there was someone stronger who would do it. But, that's not the way it works. If someone else was doing it, I wouldn't trust that it would be done right.

Right. What does that really mean?? Is it right that she had this stroke? Is it right that at times my heart just breaks with watching her? Is it right that sometimes I'm incredibly frustrated at the whole mess? Or is it right that regardless of what our past has been, I'm stepping up and doing what is in her best interest?

Even when she doesn't know it?

She left my apartment today telling me that she loves me; I told her the same thing. I could have seen her off the next morning; I could get up early and meet her at the car and kiss her one more time. But, I didn't. It's not that I don't love her, not by any stretch of the way. My fear is that to do so would only upset her, and with a very long ride ahead of her, I don't want her to start off her journey like that. Upsetting her more would not be right.

It would upset me as well for I had an equally difficult day looming; I had to call everyone and change her life permanently. It was the day I canceled her rent and utilities—the day I made the final preparations for her move; it was the day that I did all that I had to do to make her life easier. It was the day I did the right thing for her.

I stepped up to the plate and did what was right. I will be strong; I will be her champion. And I will also cry. To say that I got through the day without that aspect would be lying. It was a day

Excellence

filled with quiet. There were quiet conversations, quiet sentiments about the changes, quiet realizations that nothing will be the same, and for me, quiet tears.

Yes, sometimes the quiet is deafening, and sometimes it's really necessary to hear the voice of the Almighty guiding, counseling, and offering comfort.

A – Anticipation *July*

BETTER

I allowed myself to be sick for two days.
I'm better now.

I wasn't sure if it was something I ate, the heat in the flat, or a touch of the stomach virus. Whatever it was limited my movements to sprinting distance of the bathroom. It wasn't just that I needed to use the facilities; it was more a matter of being afraid of being too far from them in case the need arose.

It wasn't even a matter of feeling achy, tired, headachy, or just blah; it was the lack of motivation to do all the things I knew I needed to do to take really good care of myself. And it resulted in time (maybe too much) to do not much else but think.

During this thinking time, I realized just how much my life has changed over the last year. Mostly they were good changes, but changes none the less. And I couldn't help but wonder, "What's next?" I feel as though another change is about to happen; I'm finding my way—my comfort zone—in various areas of my life. Although these are also good things, I see the cycle of activity, silence, and then failure of days gone past and become afraid.

Oddly enough, what I am still afraid of is the silence. As it has normally proceeded times of failure or lost, it is difficult to trust that the silence this time is a waiting period for success. It's as if my life has slowed down to a snail's pace, and I'm finding it more and more difficult to trust the quiet. And maybe, just maybe, therein lies the lesson.

A friend of mine was visiting recently, and I listened in awe and surprise as she stated, "And this fall this will happen, and next spring that will happen, and the fall after that, this other will happen; and then the following spring…" You get the idea. I recall a time where my life was planned in 15-minute intervals for up to two years at a time. It was a time when I knew exactly what I was doing, with whom, and when. That doesn't mean it was a good thing.

Rarely do I know what I'm doing on a given afternoon, and if I wait a minute, it too will change. I have my daily to-do list, my schedule of events, and the people and goals I want to meet. But, I don't follow it, not really. It's almost as if I use it as a guide—a "would like to-do" not a "must do!" Right now, I'm on the summer schedule, and I know this fall is going to be much more schedule driven as I've eight classes I'm teaching, three that I'm taking, and then writing assignments and the standard social commitments. I'm trying to stay on schedule; really I am. I feel better when I've checked things "done" as opposed to staring at "to-do."

Yet, sometimes, between the to-do and the doing is the silence where I just feel like staying in bed all day; I have the motivation of a summer's breeze and just about as much focus. The quiet affords me the time to get so bored out of my mind that I will be forced to do what I need to do just to DO something. Like right now.

Today alone, I've two articles to write, a Hebrew lesson to review, three lesson plans to make up, and here I sit ... with my nearly cold coffee, too many cigarette butts in the ashtray, and the clock ticking away.

I've talked to some friends this morning, addressed some work-related e-mails, did my exercises, washed my face and got dressed; isn't that enough? The dishes are done, the bed is made, the laundry still needs to be folded and put away; I'd like to do some errands this afternoon or evening, and, well ... there is work that needs to be done. So why is it, that instead of doing all the stuff I should be doing, when I took a mini-break and went to the bathroom I stopped and picked up the paint and paintbrush and decided now was a good time to paint the baseboard at the front door?

Could it be, perhaps, I've spent so much time taking care of myself, of doing all the things I am required to do, that I'm up for a bigger break? Could it be that in an effort to organize my life, I've gotten myself into a rut instead? Or could it be that the silence is so very uncomfortable that I'm doing whatever I can to sustain it so it gets to a comfort level?

I know that I need to get my work done and there is the whole good feeling of having it in the "done" category; I still don't feel like doing it. I've not got the motivation, drive, or desire to get it done. It very well could be that because I don't know what I'd do once it was done, that I'm putting it off JUST so I will have something TO do. There is no logic in that.

Logic is in having all my work done so that I'll be ready for whatever else comes along. William Shakespeare is noted for saying, "The readiness is all." Readiness for what he didn't say. He also didn't say we had to do it, just be ready to do it.

So perhaps now I am ready to do what needs to be done; I'm in a better position to do it, and although I don't have the desire, I do have the readiness to do it. Or maybe not just as well.

Yes, I am better in only that I realize to do or not to do, is my choice.

When I'm seeking progress, not perfection, I won't discount the readiness with the not doing.

CONTENTMENT

I woke up in a good mood this morning.

But putting a label on what I was feeling was difficult.

Yes, I was happy, almost giddy even; I was looking forward to doing all the run-of-the-mill things I have to do today; I was excited about my date with a new suitor tonight; I was happy my homework was nearly finished; I didn't even mind THAT time of the month started early; I was enjoying the soft, gentle rain. Still, there was something else I just couldn't put my finger on.

It rather reminded me of my one and only trip to Louisville, Kentucky. I'd been invited to be a guest speaker at a writing conference and arrived on a Wednesday; the conference was to last until Sunday. About 30 minutes before the plane landed I got a "screamer." Now, for those of you who are not familiar with the term, a "screamer" is a headache caused by the change in the barometric pressure which makes you feel like the top of your head is about to explode and is so painful the only thing you want to do is "scream."

There was nothing I could take; nothing I could do. So I suffered through the conference, putting on my best smile and wearing my best manners. I awoke Sunday morning feeling something was different; very, very different. I pulled open the curtains and much to my relief it was raining; not a soft gentle rain like now, but a torrential downpour. It was then I realized what the DIFFERENT was, for the first time since I arrived, I didn't have a headache!!

And maybe, that's the difference now; I don't have the constant pain I've held for so very, very long. I don't have the fear I'm NOT okay, or I somehow don't measure up to the expectations my family have placed on me. I don't have the weight of solving everyone else's problems. I don't have the constant companion of "abandonment" issues, and I'm finally ready.

I'm ready to start living my life safe in the knowledge G-d will show me what he wants me to do, and I'll do it. I'm confident those I have chosen to be my friends are stable, and good for me. I'm happy the family members I've decided are within my circle are

July

where they need to be in this stage of their journey. I have faith that the challenges which come my way will be overcome with grace, and strength, and with an eye towards "the good of all."

I believe the word I'm looking to label this feeling is: contentment. My life is finally filled with contentment. I'm content with the various aspects of my life. I've been trying for so very long to learn how to build a relationship with another, and failing miserably, I forgot that the one of the most important relationship we have is the one with ourselves. Yes, we can take input from others and apply it as we see fit. Yes, we can read another book, watch another video, or even attend another seminar to show us the best way to live our lives. However, when we finish reading the book, watching the video, or leave the seminar, we are still all we have.

Life is like a puzzle without the box top to show us the finished product. Everyday, we get another piece of the puzzle; we pick it up, we feel the smoothness of the picture side, the roughness of the back side. We examine the shape and the edges, and we see where it fits into the pieces we've already put in place. Sometimes it fits, and we go on to the next piece. Sometimes it doesn't fit, so we put that piece to the side and still go on to the next piece. And, sometimes, we go back to the pieces which didn't fit before to see if they fit now and either take them out and replace them or just take them out all together.

Some days, we go through a bunch of pieces trying to find the one which fits best for today. Some days, we find the first piece right away, which leads to many pieces this day. Other days we may do our best and still not find a piece that fits. But at the end of the day, when we've put the pieces we've gathered together, and we like what we see, we place a light coating of the glue that holds it all together: contentment.

A life of contentment is filled with ups and downs, surprises and challenges, good stuff and bad, strengths and weaknesses. When reviewed at the end of each day, we can actually surmise, "Yes, life is grand!" Can we really ask for anything more?

Excellence
E – Excellence

SOLACE

I had no intentions of cleaning my flat today.

As it is a "money" day, my attentions are usually focused on doing activities which will result in paying the rent.

Yet, as I went to get a cup of coffee, I noticed the trash needed to be taken out; as I went to get dressed, I noticed there were clothes which needed to be folded and put away; as I walked into the dressing room, I noticed the tile was in need of attention. As I pride myself in keeping my flat in excellent condition, I realized this did not constitute my definition of excellence.

So, it was without malice that I collected the trash, folded and put away the clothes, dusted the tile, and for good measure, did a load of rugs, changed the kitty litter box, started the dishwasher, and wiped down all the counters.

There is something about doing menial tasks which calms the mind; it's like a break from the real world, but refreshing as well. I realized as I folded the clothes on the kitchen counter that I could hear the washer filling and the dishwasher running, and I took solace in the fact that I was not only multi-tasking, but doing that which needed to be done to sustain my quality of life.

Simple things actually—little bits of joy at smelling the freshness of the fabric softener, feeling the fluffiness of the towels, standing on a clean kitchen floor, listening to the rhythm of the washer, enjoying the site of clean surfaces, tasting the sips in between from a good cup of coffee, and just being.

I had wanted to find a time when I could just stand still and breathe; I never dreamed I'd find it folding clothes in my kitchen on a money day. Yep, sometimes life surprises you, and they are excellent surprises at that.

SUMMARY

As you focused on GRACE this month, did you see a parallel to an issue in your own life? The following ten questions may help you gain new perspective on how to manage it.

Questions to ponder:

1. Is this issue bigger than me?

2. What is my part in resolving the issue?

3. Is now the right time?

4. What's stopping me?

5. How do I remove the barriers?

6. What resources will I need to get started?

7. What resources do I have?

Excellence
Answers to Act on:

8. What isn't working?

9. What is working?

10. What's the next step?

To do List:

August

FIERCE
(Fabulous and Fearless)

August is a month of fierceness. No reason to be afraid of what the future holds. You are courageous and ready to face the challenges. During this time of boldness, focus on …

G   for GIRLY
R   for RELATIONSHIPS
A   for APRECIATION
C   for CHARACTER
E   for EVEN

Fierce
G – Girly

PINK IS A STATE OF MIND

He told me I looked good in pink.
I was surprised to discover, he was right.

My basic colors for as long as I can recall have been red, white, or some shade of black. Except for my standard denim blue jeans, those were the colors in my closet. I'm a simple girl when it comes to wardrobes: classic designs, straight lines, well-fitting, and easy to mix and match. I was certain to buy only natural fibers (cottons, wools, silks, denim) as I just couldn't breath wearing the poly-whatevers, and my skin would usually break out in a rash within minutes when I chanced it. They tell me it's part of my allergies, but I'm thinking it may also be a matter of preference. Oh sure, every once in a while I'd go to the Soulard Market or the shop on Beale Street and pick up an item or two of ethnic origin which was bold, bright, highly patterned and looked great on me. But, for the most part, everything in my closet can go with everything else.

Why I even bought the hot pink, boat neck, cotton top was beyond me. It probably had something to do with my daughter-in-law convincing me I needed to break out of my color-shell. His comment had been in passing, but I still found it flattering. That was about two years ago.

I'm still dealing with my pink situation; although I've added pastel pink tank tops, a very soft pink sweater suit, and several pink sleeveless blouses to my wardrobe, I still wonder if I am a "pink" kind of gal, or more importantly, if I should be.

There is something about the color pink that brings out the softer side of me; I used to believe this was a weakness. I'm not so sure anymore. There has always been an incredible strength to my clothing choices; I not only dress for the occasion, but for the image I want to portray. Usually, my image is one of confidence, knowledge, being well-educated and well-traveled. There is a certain air about me that comes off as East-coast-together—a grace and chic which has been well developed. My hair is styled well; my nails are sporting a natural French manicure; my stiletto heels are highly shined. This image suites me well for business.

August

But, perhaps, it is not so well suited for my personal life, and maybe, therein lays the problem.

The softer side of me is what I call my "baby girl" side; she is compassionate, passionate, funny, silly, a little bit shy, and very much into intimacy and gentle touches. She can also throw a temper tantrum with the best of them and act badly when she doesn't get what she wants. The same man who told me I looked good in pink is the one who uncovered this side of me. She has been hurt a great deal over the years, and for her safety hid behind the bolder, more aggressive, Dragon Lady side of me. In business, and other situations, this has served me well. But I'm wondering, when it comes to personal relationships, is this the preferred image?

My best girlfriend told me yesterday to start doing the opposite of what I've done in the past to see if I could get better results in the dating arena. Maybe it's not only in the actions but also in the image.

If I have been using the strength of my business image to start a personal relationship, it's no wonder I scare the daylights out of men before they even have a chance to get to know me. It is no secret that when it comes to business and business relationships, I truly am the strong, formidable force of the Dragon Lady. It's not a matter of being mean and rude but of being fair, honest, not backing down, laying it on the line, and being tenacious.

Wow. As I read this I can't help but be shocked! What man in his right mind would want to DATE a woman like that? None that I've known, that's for sure and for certain. It almost sounds like I'm being ... a ... man.

Hmm. Well now, there's a thought.

As I look back over my life, I see that my strength in my marriage and in my business has been to be the strong one: to make the hard decisions, stand by my word, and do what had to be done at the time.

My dating life reflects this in spades. I remember one man, who I only dated once, telling me he didn't want to fight his way through the cold, hard exterior to find the softer side of me. I didn't think much of it at the time; but, now that I do, he does have a point.

Which brings me to the point of asking, if what I've done this far hasn't worked, what would be the harm in flipping the images? If showing the strong side of me has driven them away, what if I showed the softer side first? I'm willing to admit the reason I've not done this before is because my softer side has been hurt so many times. But, is she hurting any less this way?

If I've always considered the softer side to be the prize of getting through the outer shell, what if I turned it around? What if the prize was in finding the strong, smart, well traveled side instead? Would this be deceitful? Would I be selling someone a bill of goods that were false? Or, would I be attracting more bees with honey than vinegar?

Up until about three years ago, my hair color was black. I mean coal, midnight black. It had been that way since before my youngest son was born, and to be honest he didn't think I'd ever had any other color. I decided to go blonde, and it took me the better part of a year to do so; this was not an easy process, and I went through several shades of black-brown-red-dirty blonde and streaks of each at the same time to get there. Now, according to the box, my hair color is Ultra Light Natural Blonde. Whether I enjoy the process or not, I recolor it every two to three weeks just to keep it that color. I also color my eyebrows to a bit darker blonde just to complete the look. I LOVE it.

One of the unexpected surprises in doing this was the way the hair color affects my eye color. My eyes used to be dark brown; they are now hazel. The blonde also darkens my tan, and that's not a bad thing at all. I didn't know these changes would happen, but still, they fit with the hair color.

Ah, therein lays the key to confusion. If I've changed the outside to be blonde and soft but my actions are still strong and smart, then I need to change the rest of the image to fit the softer side.

There is a hair color commercial that says something like, "When you want to re-invent yourself, start from the top down." I did this – for the most part. Now, I just need to change the actions and the clothes to fit. I realize in making these changes, it's not selling someone a bill of goods to show one side of ourselves; it's buying us time to get to know each other, to get to know the other parts; and it's allowing ourselves the time to uncover all of the sides of ourselves together. I have to realize I don't always need to be strong, smart and together; it is okay to be soft and gentle and let a

August

man believe that I do need him to be the man—the hero. There is no weakness in letting another be strong.

When I finish writing this I'm changing my standard French manicure to a colored look. The name on the bottle is: baby pink. ☺

KENNEL CLUB

I thought they were bad boys.

I realize they were just puppies.

A new friend of mine yelled at me, well, maybe "yelled at me" is a bit harsh where rocked my world would be more appropriate. Normally this is not a reaction I elicit from people I've just started befriending.

As one thing led to another in our first conversation, my last serious relationship became the topic. Yes, I gushed about how I really liked him, how he was the ideal man in appearance, but his baggage...my goodness the baggage was just too tough.

In other words, she surmised, he messed on your carpet.

Her words stopped me in mid-sentence.

She went on to explain that he was just a puppy; at the end of the day, the fact was he messed on my carpet.

Long after our conversation ended, I thought about her analogy. Was she right? Were the men in my life really nothing more than puppies?

Hmm. There were basically three men who walked through my life where this analogy would fit. Yes, they were cute, cuddly, ever so much fun to play with, but they messed on my carpet, peed on my sofa, and chewed up my shoes.

The first puppy was adorable, in a Heinz 57 kind of way. He would come when summoned, but only when summoned; he could play with the best of them. But when he got upset, well, he'd throw a temper tantrum and really wreak havoc on the furniture. He refused to be paper trained and really believed I should love him just the way he was, bad manners and all.

The second was a real junk yard dog; he'd bring the ball to me, tease me with a game of catch, but when I threw the ball, he'd not retrieve it. Sure, like Lucy and her football, there was always the promise of a real game; but when it came down to it, he'd pull the ball away at a critical moment, and I'd fall flat on my back. He wasn't incredibly cute, but he could make me feel safe with the best of them. He was territorial, and bulky, and sometimes comfortable

August

to be around. However, he wandered into any bed that was available, would take whatever was given, and gave little in return.

The third was the pedigreed lost puppy wanting to come home. He was cute, and needy, and ever so helpless that my heart just went out to him. I didn't realize how hard he could bite until he did. Sure, he'd go away for a bit, and then come back again. He'd return to his former master only to come running back to where he knew there was comfort: a warm bed, a hot meal, and a belly-scratch. Did I mention someone to clean up his messes? Maybe I didn't.

This brings me to another level of understanding. If they were the puppies, was I the master or just the kennel? In this relationship, what was my role?

Hmm. I fed them, gave them fresh water, took them out for a daily walk, cleaned up after their messes, tried my best to paper train them and give them good manners. Strangely, I loved them despite the time, trouble, and resources I used, some may say wasted.

But, still, they messed on my carpet, peed on my sofa, and chewed on my shoes.

Is it their fault that this happened, or mine?

I've been thinking about getting a puppy; not just any puppy, but a Cavalier King Charles Spaniel. You are probably unfamiliar with the breed, as I was until I took one of those "Chose a pet that's right for you" online quizzes which was rather like filling out one of those on line dating profiles. The dogs have a long line of good English breeding, are low maintenance, easy to get along with, they are just the right size for my home, spontaneous, loving, and cute as a button.

On the advice of the same puppy site, I did some checking around to find a "quality" puppy farm; not knowing what a "quality" puppy farm even consisted of, I was grateful for the list of questions I needed to ask of the breeder. And so it was that I came upon a puppy name Harley; he had me at the name as my favorite motor cycle is of the same name. Calling the breeder I quickly got the sense that theirs was, in fact, a "quality" puppy farm.

Okay, I had the money; she had the puppy. So, why didn't I buy him?

Fierce

Maybe it was when she said, "You know you'll have to train him to use the paper." I not only didn't know I HAD to do this; I had no idea of HOW to do this.

"You also have to keep him in a room with a tile floor until he learns to use the paper." Okay, I've got a bathroom, dressing room and kitchen for that.

"You also have to train him as to what furniture he can and can't get on; who he can bark at and who he can't, and don't forget when he's allowed to bark." Bark? He barks? How long can my neighbors stand for him to bark?

"Then there's the daily 20-minute walks that you have to give him." Twenty minute walks? Does that include or is it in addition to the seven flights of stairs just to get to the dog run?

"Don't forget, he'll need his shots every six weeks." That's doable, I think to myself. "And we've got his records so you'll have to find a good vet in your neighborhood to transfer the records to." Oh. I hadn't thought of that. Will my cat's vet work? I didn't know.

"If you use him for breeding he'll be fine; if not you need to think about getting him ... you know." Breeding? How do you breed dogs?

"You do have a patio where he can just go outside for a few minutes three or four times a day, right?" Well, yeah, but it's three stories up and will have to be fixed so he can't fall or jump off.

At this point I heaved a heavy sigh. She heard this. "You know," she said, not unkindly, "I think what you need is a dog; not a puppy." There's a difference?

"Oh," say I meekly.

"Yes," she said. "A dog has already been trained, has his manners, knows how to use the paper, understands his role as primary comfort giver, and will actually protect you as second nature. We can discuss the breeding issue later."

"I don't have to do any of those other things?"

"No," she said. "You feed him, give him fresh water, take him for daily walks, and play with him. If you want, I'll train him for you; and when you're both ready, he'll be yours."

I'm guessing what she meant was when he'd grown up and I was willing to provide basic maintenance and the fun stuff.

This is how the two lines of thought—men and puppies—converged.

August

I wanted to find a man, in dog speak, who was loyal, faithful, paper trained, would keep me safe, is ever so glad to see me at the end of the day and best of all, is my friend to the very end. In the man relationship, I want the comfort level that comes with the quiet times, lying on the parlor bed, watching a movie, whispering concerns or bits of nothing, touching and being touched, and the security that comes with the quiet.

The real problem with puppies is that women, naturally, have this overwhelming need to take care of them -- and we confuse love with pity. We think fulfilling all of their needs is love, and it isn't; it's maintenance.

At the end of the day, no matter what you've given them, a puppy will still mess on your carpet. A dog simply wants his food, fresh water, a quick walk, and a belly scratch. This is something I can happily provide.

Come to think of it, it's a lot like what I'm looking for too.

Fierce
A – Appreciation

THE LITTLE THINGS

Thank you, Lord, for all the good things in my life.
Thank you also, for the bad.

Such has been my prayer on more than one occasion; fact is, on more occasions than I readily admit. Like most people, I find the good things are easy to be thankful for, grateful and appreciative for even. The bad things have a way of making me stop and think, and look – sometimes look really hard – to find the good things in them.

By all accounts, my life has been a series of misadventures for the last 18 months. I might add, I've analyzed them to the nth degree and can find no part of mine in the causing of these events. I have, however, realized that in most of these cases I've been asked to step up to the plate, to make the hard decisions, to offer comfort and support to those who were at the center of the various situations.

It is almost as if I've been a supporting character in a theatrical production. I didn't cause the event, I can fix it to the best of my abilities, and I do take personal responsibility to do so. However, I'm finding that when the bad things happen, there seems to be an "If/Then" relationship that comes out of them which helps balance the scales between the bad thing and the good things.

For a dramatic example, IF my mother had not had a stroke, THEN my siblings and I would not have had the FABULOUS opportunity of repairing our relationships and coming to the healthiest place we've ever been in. Now, at first blush this may seem like an extreme measure to get a small distance; but, once you take into consideration that we were dealing with 45 plus years of a dysfunctional family and horrific past encounters, it is nothing short of a miracle that we've gotten here.

This was like dropping a pebble in a pond; the ripples were far, wide, deep and very necessary to get us to this good place. It was like one really big bad thing happened, and hundreds of really good things occurred because of it. I jumped from the bad thing to the end result of a good thing, and left out all the little things in between. There were dozens of GOOD little things from finding myself in a Catholic hospital and having people come up to me and

August

strike up a conversation about Judaism, to actually having the time and money to make all the trips I made back and forth, to having my sister call me and wail at the world because she finally felt comfortable in doing so, to seeing the hand of G-d bless every single step of this journey in ways that are incomprehensible.

I appreciate all the little things G-d has done to help me and my family. I know the good things could not have happened without the bad things happening. I know drastic measures HAD to be taken to make my family of origin finally work.

I am grateful for the seemingly bad things. Such as, I am grateful that I didn't have a full time job, as I wouldn't have been able to help my mom and do all the things she can no longer do for herself and all the things that had to be done so that she is in a very good place. I am grateful that I didn't have a full semester of classes as I wouldn't have had the time to go and see her, help her move, get her settled and deal with the mountains of paperwork. Just as well, I am grateful for the really good things. I appreciate the kindness and generosity of my friends and family who have blessed me with comfort and support as I couldn't have done it without them. I am grateful for the strangers along the way who did whatever they could to help us all get to this good place.

Most of all, I'm grateful and appreciative of G-d, who's mighty hand made it all possible. These things, in and of themselves, are miracles ... made up of dozens of little miracles along the way; little things that make up a life.

C – Character

IDENTITY

I did it because he did.

And this is a good thing, how?

I guess it would be a different story if I believed the actions of another were acceptable or even better than my own, but they weren't. As I was driving home this morning from a very early appointment that I actually kept, I started thinking about the way I think and how sometimes I adopt the thinking habits of others.

It is said that birds of a feather flock together, but, what if they don't? What if said birds all just live in the same coup, or take the same route south, or better still, just congregate at the same bird feeder for no other reason than circumstances? And what if, just by being together, they take on the characteristics of others which may not be true to themselves?

The whole point here is that when thinking about the way I think, and then the actions I take on those thoughts, I realized sometimes I am being true to myself, and other times not so much.

I don't know why I got to thinking about the relationship with my youngest son and the various times I would say something hurtful, mean, or what I would deem inappropriate, and then—worst of possible worse sins—cop out and say, "I'm just kidding." The reality was, for whatever reason, I'd been hanging around his father too much at the time, and I had picked up on his method of thinking—one I might admit that I don't subscribe to as a general rule.

His father was the type of person who not only believed every Junk Science finding that came out, but also believed that whatever it was would suddenly apply to him, me, or the kids. If there was anything that could go wrong, he'd take it out exponentially to the umpteenth degree, and suddenly it would be a crisis.

Needless to say, I don't watch the news. It's not so much that I like living in my hovel or feel it necessary to cower under a rock, but to be perfectly honest, I don't *want* to know. Every time I turn on the news, it's bad news. I feel I have enough "junk" in my own life; I don't need to clutter it with the "junk" of others.

August

    This all leads back to the way I think and act. At what point do I either accept the behavior of others, or adopt it, or, take a risk of saying something and possibly ending a relationship? I don't know; what I do know is I fear I will be pushing my relationships away.

    It's frustrating, maddening even; but, there is a part of me that says I need to set some boundaries; not lose myself, but clarify my relationship.

    I realize in my marriage I accepted everything my ex was willing to give me; I compromised myself, our relationship, and adapted as was necessary to survive on a daily basis. My best guy friend told me there was no blame to be laid for my actions as, "Survival trumps everything; you did what you had to do to survive."

    Yet now, it is a different story altogether. At what point do I lose my identity by adopting their modes of behavior to satisfy the needs of another? I don't know, but I feel like each compromise along the way is one step closer to doing the same thing with my relationships as I did with my ex; I sacrifice who I am for who they want me to be. This doesn't work for me. It may suffice for a while, but then I get fed up with it and walk away. It took me thirty-one years to walk the first time; I admit it was a long time in coming. But, do I really want to take that long again? I'm guessing no.

    I'm always one to look at the potential in something; I find good in every situation, and I am not above working for this possible good. To be true to myself, and ONLY myself, it would behoove me to just wait out issues and see; and while I'm waiting, be happy for the good place my relationships have reached. This may also be giving me the time to figure out just what it is that I do want. They tell me the true sign of being an adult is the ability to wait for what we want and not expect instant gratification. This being said, the possibilities for later is where my thinking lies.

Fierce
E – Even

CENTERED

We all know people who are selfish.

I'd like to believe I'm not one of them.

Selfishness has gotten some pretty bad press over the years. It's gone from a term meaning "looking after own desires" to "concerned with your own interests, needs, and wishes while ignoring those of others". To be selfish now means to do whatever it takes to get your own way regardless of who you have to hurt or how badly you have to act to get it.

It's now a matter of being controlling, manipulative, deceitful and untrustworthy. Hmm, those words could all be used to describe me at one point or another in my life. I would be quick to point out, at the time, that my heart was in the right place; that the ends DID justify the means; that my actions were for the greater good. So goes the self-justification for bad actions, regardless of the intent.

Arguments could be made that these actions were fueled by fear, or past pain, or maybe even ignorance; one was afraid of losing, so they became selfish to hedge their bet; one was afraid of being hurt again so one became selfish to put a wall around themselves; or maybe, just maybe, one never grew up enough to learn how not to be selfish.

I'd like to think that through fear and pain and, yes, even ignorance, I've learned how not to be selfish but instead to be centered.

I've a best girlfriend who never ceases to be amazed at just how open and honest and …well…venerable I am when it comes to matters of the heart. 'Tis true, my last relationship was devastating when it ended; it was painful to endure when it was in full force, and there were lessons aplenty to learn throughout. I learned how to be strong with someone, and for someone, and in the end…against someone.

I was selfish in this last relationship in that I wanted to control it, force it to be what I wanted it to be, and in the end…lost it. Oh, I know it wasn't all my fault, and I've no real regrets for the lessons I learned about being patient, strong, and having faith were worth the

August

pain; but, there is still a part of me that wants the good stuff back. Perhaps it will happen; a girl can only hope.

There is a cycle of confusion prevalent here: the cycle between being selfish, being centered, and being somewhere in between. On the one hand, we are selfish when we do what we need to do to get what we want; on the other hand we stay centered in our everyday lives and let the relationship flow as it will; and somewhere in between, we deal with all the emotions which are a result of this middle ground.

What we have right now is all we have. Is it better to spend the time trying to control and manipulate the situation to get what we think we want? Or is it better to take baby steps forward in all the other areas of our lives while we wait and see where that area leads?

I would like to think that being centered is being strong enough to deal with all of life's little ups and downs without too much drama—having the ability to go after what we want without too much fear—but also knowing where the line is between what we can control and what we can't and stopping before we cross that line. Yes, it is quite like the serenity prayer, with one big difference: the difference between change and control. I will grant that many can't see the difference, but to me, change simply means to "make different" and control means "to exercise power or authority over something or someone." It is a difference in mindset; one means that we accept our powerlessness; the other means we mistakenly think we have the power in the first place.

We can't "change" a red light to green; we can easily accept this. While we cannot "control" another person, however, we mistakenly think we can and as such set out on a self-defeating journey.

I'd like to think that the difference between being selfish and being centered lies in the number of apologies we need to issue for our bad behavior. It's one thing to make an honest mistake, say we are sorry for it, make amends, and not do it again. It's quite another to act badly while trying to control or manipulate another and then feel the embarrassment for those actions. Perhaps that is where the true meaning of the serenity prayer lies; accepting that which we can not change, changing that which we can, wisdom to know the difference, and living so that we do not need to apologize.

SUMMARY

As you focused on GRACE this month, did you see a parallel to an issue in your own life? The following ten questions may help you gain new perspective on how to manage it.

Questions to ponder:

1. Is this issue bigger than me?

2. What is my part in resolving the issue?

3. Is now the right time?

4. What's stopping me?

5. How do I remove the barriers?

6. What resources will I need to get started?

7. What resources do I have?

August

Answers to Act on:

8. What isn't working?

9. What is working?

10. What's the next step?

To do List:

Fierce

September

FAITH AND RE-EVALUATION

September is a month of faith and re-evaluation. When things are going well, it's never a bad time to review your life and examine your beliefs. During this time of questioning, focus on …

- **G**   for G-D
- **R**   for REASON
- **A**   for ASSESSMENT
- **C**   for COPING
- **E**   for ENCOURAGEMENT

Faith and Re-evaluation
G – G-d

LIMITS

My grandchildren each think I am *only* theirs.

So, why do I think of G-d in the same way?

As I sit here, it's 11 p.m., and my nerves are shot. Although it's been a long day, the reason my nerves are shot is because there has been a terrible storm, and it has left my youngest son in the dark with no heat. The worst part is there is nothing I can do about it. The hotels are full or without power; the shelters are small and full; there is no place else he can go.

He thinks it's no big deal as he figures he and his girlfriend are in the house, and it's well insulated. They can dress in layers, and they've got all the clothes and blankets they need to keep them warm.

I'm not so sure.

Actually, I wasn't even remotely okay with this until without warning my Hebrew instructor called to ask if I was going to brave the storm in the morning for our meeting; I said I wasn't going anywhere unless school wasn't called the next day, and I would have to go to work.

She asked if I was okay; I told her no and WHY I wasn't okay.

It was then that she related her three-week stay in Chicago, in a bad apartment, during one of the worst times of the winter, and how she survived it without incident with lots of layers, head coverings, and clean socks. She then assured me my son would be fine if he dressed for it, and that all would be well.

It would be quite the adventure for him and something he could brag about later to his children and grandchildren.

So, why am I so afraid for him?

My friend said because he's my son, he's only 23, and I think I know what's better for him than he does. She was right. It struck me that I was afraid for him because I'd come so very close to losing him so many times before that I didn't want to risk losing him again; she assured me I wasn't in any danger of that happening.

Quite some time after we talked, and I talked again with my son confirming the dressing code, I said a prayer asking G-d to watch over him and keep him safe.

September

It suddenly didn't feel like I was asking the Almighty to take care of my beloved, but that I was telling Him to do something I couldn't. This did not sit well with me at all.

Then I realized why. His answer was, "As if I wouldn't??"

Why is it when I think of G-d, I think He is *only* mine? When I visit my grandchildren, each of them wants to be in my lap, read them a tale first, to show them in some way that I am ONLY theirs, that I love THEM best. But, I have limits, G-d doesn't. I can only be at one place at a one time; He can be everywhere at once. I can only do one (maybe three) things at one time; He can do endless things all the time. I get tired; He doesn't.

So, I'm back to my question: why do I feel when G-d is with me He ISN'T with someone else? Am I so arrogant as to believe I am the MOST important person in the universe? No. Is it maybe, just maybe, because I know I have limits and I feel He is ALWAYS with me, so I don't get that He can be somewhere else as well?

I've seen Him work in my son's life time and time again; so why wouldn't he now? The truth is He will work in my son's life.

Is this maybe His way of teaching me that He doesn't have limits and that He can be with me AND everyone else in the world?

There is a point I am dancing around here and have been for the last three paragraphs. I've set a standard for the responsibilities in my life; they are three questions:

1. Did I break it?
2. Can I fix it?
3. Is it my responsibility to do so?

The point is this, if I am to believe these questions hold true for all of my situations in life, can they hold true for the Almighty as well?

If I look at the situation, I will quickly see I didn't cause the storm that knocked out half the power in the town my son lives in; I certainly can't fix it; so it is not my responsibility.

Looking closer, I will contend G-d did allow the storm; He can fix it; so it is His responsibility? I put a question mark here, because I'm not sure. Maybe it's because I'm suddenly confused.

Storms happen; I can't fix them, and in this instance, I can't even make it better; so perhaps it is ONLY G-d who can fix it, guide the hands of the power company worker to make the right repairs,

Faith and Re-evaluation

and keep my son and others safe and warm and happy in the knowledge that all will be well.

So maybe this is one of those situations where G-d's will be done comes into play. Maybe I need to know that I am NOT the creator of the universe, that I truly am only along for the ride; and that I need to realize when G-d is with me, He is also with all I hold dear.

As a codependent, I somehow feel that everything is my responsibility, that all problems I encounter are either my fault or up to me to fix. But, if I could do that—I mean really, REALLY do that—wouldn't I have to BE G-d?? I'm NOT G-d; I'm only human; I have limits; I have finite resources.

But, maybe what we really need above all is the faith that as we are walking the path He put us on, and He's preparing us and helping us walk, He's doing the same with everyone else.

I need to realize that the Almighty is NOT just my G-d; He is EVERYONE'S G-d. As such, He's doing for them precisely what He's doing for me. And as a human, I need to understand that I can't do His job; and He really does it so much better than I ever could.

R – Reason

September

DON'T ...

I've often contended that I was never a girly-girl.

I realize now I was lying to myself.

There are some women who just ooze femininity; my oldest granddaughter is one of them. I was not. I use the word "was" instead of "am" for a very important reason: I am one now, and I wasn't then.

I will contend I've never much cared for dolls; I was always more interested in how they were made or how they worked as opposed to dressing them. I can throw a mean tea party, make wonderful cakes in my Easy Bake Oven™, and can sew a quilt with the best of them.

So why is it, do you think, I've always been more inclined to explore the Tom Boy aspects of my character than to embrace my feminine side? Don't.

"Don't be such a sissy."

"Don't take it personally."

"Don't be so emotional; you need to be strong so some man doesn't walk all over you."

And my personal favorite, "Young lady, if you don't stop crying this instant I'll give you a reason to cry."

It seems to me if I was crying I *had* a good reason, else I wouldn't *be* crying, and I didn't need another reason; they didn't see it quite that way. Whatever reason I had to be crying was not acceptable to them, so they felt the need to give me a reason that they thought *was* acceptable.

Growing up, I realized I couldn't show my emotions as those around me would judge them, criticize them, and feel the need to dictate just what emotions I should be feeling at the time. It didn't help that I married a man who bought into this concept and took on the role my parents had vacated.

Each time I acted like a girl, let alone a girly-girl, by crying, I was told "don't," and it was reinforced with a good deal of pain. It wasn't just for crying from physical pain; it was also anger, fear, vulnerability, and a host of other emotions including joy at the simple things, excitement, and silliness. I formed barriers that kept

Faith and Re-evaluation

in all the bad and kept out all the good. These are not the kind of barriers anyone should have, let alone a child.

There is a certain perceived helplessness that comes with femininity; a certain quality that isn't a neediness but a vulnerability that comes with being a woman; a certain joy that comes with being with the one who touches our soul that we can't find by ourselves. I miss this terribly.

There is also a level of owning our emotions which comes with the package too: we are strong enough to be weak; we are afraid enough to be brave; we are jaded enough to be sensitive: we are venerable enough to trust; we are reasonable to cry. We have hope that the good guy really does win; good does overcome evil; that fairy tales really do come true and there is magic around every corner. We trust in the journey, ever aware that the Almighty is looking out for us, and we are free to feel what we feel whenever we feel it; no reasons needed.

Our emotions are ours and ours alone. We don't need a reason to have them. I hope I may keep the freedom and the courage to express them. I like being a girly-girl, and I'm realizing I am now strong enough to be one.

A – Assessment

September

SET IN STONE

My dreams were never set in stone.
I'm thinking maybe they should have been.
My forty-ninth birthday is one I'm facing with trepidation. It's a strange birthday for me; it falls on a Sabbath, is my 7/7 year, and a sabbatical year. It begins with the eve of the only blue moon this year, and above all, it is my year of great change.

I'm wondering though, could it not also be a year of great dreams? Could the forthcoming changes be all the changes I need to make—do all the things I need to do—to realize my dreams? It's no longer a matter of "making do" with my life revolving around my children, my business, or my husband, and their wants and needs being at the forefront as it has been in years gone past.

I'm in a very good place right now, rather like the starting line of a very important journey. I would say race, but I don't see a finish line or a need to rush; I just see a trail that leads to very good things. It's also a starting point where many of the issues which took my focus before don't anymore. It's as if I've finally gotten to the place where I have all the pieces to the puzzle of my life in the box.

Now I need to figure out what those pieces look like and how they fit together. My best guy friend told me the easiest way to do this is to break every thing down into "Needs" and "Wants" and when doing so not to limit the "Needs" to basic survival issues, but also to include the quality of life measures I want to become a part of my life.

With this set of criteria, I'm guessing my needs would fall into two categories: today and tomorrow. Today's needs would be the every day survival needs: air, water, food, shelter, clothing, transportation, AND human interaction. Tomorrow's needs would be the needs I want to start on today to make my dreams a reality. They are also the elements I want to incorporate into my life to make me the type of person I want to become—the elements I need to add to start living my "dream" life.

With change comes fear or excitement. Sometimes I find it hard to tell the difference. I normally find when my blood pressure

Faith and Re-evaluation

goes up, I have to ask myself: What are you afraid of? When the answer comes back, "Nothing", then I know I am excited, not afraid.

I'm not accustomed to taking care of only me; this last year has shown me that unless I do take care of myself first, I can't take care of anyone else. Perhaps this next year will show me that I don't NEED to take care of anyone else; they can do just fine on their own; my own self-worth is NOT tied to how many people I take care of, but how many people I let take care of themselves. This year will be a year of great change. But suddenly, I can't see this as being a bad thing in any language.

C – Coping

FAITH

Faith is easy.
In the good times, we feel there is no need to have it.
But, in the bad times it's all that we have to hold on to.

I've been going through a bad patch lately; seems there's more bills than money; every thing I touched turned to sand; I found myself in the position where my rent was due, my cars were staring repossession in the face, my insurance and cell phone payments were on the verge of cancellation, and the check I deposited to cover all of them, had a stop payment attached to it. The client changed his mind and decided he didn't want my services after all. It would have been nice to know that before I wrote the checks.

I thought the sudden income was a G-d send: a miracle. But, it sent me into a level of frustration, depression, and desperation that I've never known. I cried out to all I knew searching for help. There was none to be found. I tried loans, pleadings, calling clients for past due bills; there was nothing to come.

I had been on my knees, had done what I thought I needed to do, but still, no solution was in sight.

About 3:30 on my Black Friday my youngest son called me. We chatted for a few minutes when he asked if he'd woken me. I said no. He asked me what was wrong. The dam burst, and all the hurt, frustration, and desperation came flooding out. He told me how sorry he was; I told him if I didn't do something very quickly, my cars were going to be repossessed, and I would have no home. He told me that I could always live with him. I thanked him and smiled at his attempt to make the situation better. He told me that he just got his paycheck, and if it would help he would give me $300. I chuckled and told him that it wouldn't help when I need $2,500 by five o'clock that day. We ended the conversation, telling each other that we loved the other.

He called back a few minutes later. I was talking to another friend on the other line and asked him what he needed. He said he had just one quick question: could he take money from a credit card and put it in my checking account? I told him that yes, it could be done. He asked which account it was, and I told him. But, I wasn't

Faith and Re-evaluation

paying attention. He told me he would call me right back. I blew him off.

About 45 minutes went by, and he called yet again. By this time I was at the end of my frustration rope, and his ever cheery voice was almost like fingernails on a chalk board. "Whacha need, baby doll?" I asked him and sighed at the same time.

"Nothing," he said. "I just wanted to call you and let you know you're taken care of."

I was confused. "What?"

"It's taken care of. You've got your apartment and the cars for another month."

I was still confused. "What are you talking about?"

"Momma," he whispered, "I just put $2,500 cash into your checking account."

I was speechless. I couldn't breathe. I started to shake. "What did you say?" I whispered.

"I just wanted to help my momma for all the things she's done for me," he said. I could hear the smile in his voice; I could hear the pride; I could hear the small boy who had somehow become a man in the span of 90 minutes.

"I don't know how to thank you," I said, then broke into tears.

"Shh, momma, a little bit each month would be nice!" he said then laughed.

"How in the name of all that's holy did you pull that off?" I exclaimed in astonishment.

He told me how he first went to his father (which was akin to having teeth pulled with no Novocain) to borrow the money; he didn't have it, but did have a spare $100. So, he went to his girlfriend's grandfather, and got a cash advance.

"Baby doll," I whispered, the tears streaming down my face, "I don't know how I could ever repay this favor."

He got stern with me. "By getting back on your feet; by getting back up to where I know you belong."

We talked for quite some time after that, our conversation broken by my tears. I had gotten to the point where my son was helping me. I've only been in this position two other times in my life. I didn't like it then, and I hated it now. In a strange way, his stern words were motivating for me. They made me start to mentally plan how to do just what he asked. It was as if I was failing by myself,

September

but because my *son* demanded that I get back to where I belonged, I was suddenly driven to not let *him* down.

I sat for a long time after we hung up, just thinking. A scripture I'd read the week before said, "They will suffer for a little while, and then G-d will come just in time."

And isn't this just what He'd done; come just in time? When all seemed lost, help arrived from the most unexpected place.

Yet, somehow this was a familiar situation. Time and again, when I needed something, when I needed help, it would be there. I didn't plan it that way; I didn't know where the help would come from; it would just arrive.

So, if past experience should teach us the lessons for future encounters, where was my faith that this time would be no different? What lesson was I supposed to be learning? Then I realized that sometimes His lessons come in multiple forms. In this case it wasn't just the money to pay the bills; it was also a motivation—a push over the hump of our own making, a swift kick to get us out of our rut, a reason besides ourselves to succeed, to do what we have to do, so as to not disappoint another. In turn, not disappointing Him, but rising to the occasion and pleasing Him.

A friend of mine told me that we have to have faith in the unknown because to not would mean that everything we'd done to this point was wasted.

So, if G-d got me this apartment and both of my cars and made it possible for me to have all that I do have, why would I even consider the possibility that he would take it away from me?

Where was MY faith?

What IS faith?

If you ask my best guy friend, he'd say, "Faith is a form of trust that allows one to accept that which seems impossible as being eminently feasible." Good definition. Pretty broad, but good none the less; and isn't faith in and of itself broad?

We have faith in ourselves.

We have faith that all will work out to our best interests.

We have faith that G-d has a plan.

We have faith that we are living according to His plans.

So, why is it, at the break of dawn on our darkest days, our faith waivers? We are unsure if we are going to make it through this troubled day. We are suddenly consumed with fear, dread, and uncertainty.

Faith and Re-evaluation

Is it because our faith is weak? Is it because we are so arrogant to believe that because WE can't see the solution that the Almighty can't? Or is it because we are human, and as humans, we are children compared to the Almighty? As children we get afraid of the dark; we are terrified of the thunder and lightening storm; we are scared silly of the boogey man in the closet.

As our loving father, He comes to us, holds us tight, turns on the light, and opens the closet door to show there is nothing to fear. He sits with us, rocking us lovingly, compassionately, calming us; then He kisses us on the forehead, tucks us in, and stays with us until we are fast asleep. I can almost see Him shaking His head as He whispers, "Dear child, will you never learn?"

I'd like to believe that He gives us these challenges to allow others in our lives a chance to be the hero, to time and again prove that whatever challenge He brings us, He will also see us through. He will teach us the lessons we need to learn to do His work.

I do believe He knows this is neither the first nor the last time that He will need to come to my aid. Like the good father He is, He will be there. I've often said that just because I don't know the reason for something happening doesn't mean there isn't one. I'm beginning to believe that just because I don't see a solution, doesn't mean there isn't one. As G-d knows the reason, He also knows the solution. I really like that.

E – Encouragement

September

THE STRUGGLE TO NOT STRUGGLE

I don't get mad very often.

So it struck me as odd that I would become enraged at G-d.

It was a typical Friday afternoon, if there is such an animal in my life. I'd gotten around for the day and gone into work for a couple of classes. I was happy that I had gas in the car, smokes in the pantry, food in the fridge, and all the trappings to keep my cat happy. So it was I was enjoying a late rainy afternoon nap when a friend of mine came over, waking me in the process.

It was all good that she did as we've a pretty open-door policy; when we need the other, the door is open. She stayed only but a few minutes at a time when my only task was getting the mail and then getting ready for Temple.

The mail ... sigh. That's an understatement. I'd been waiting since August for this mail run; the simple truth was I was expecting my student loan check. The same check that would pay for my divorce, my debt to mom, two car payments, the catch up rent payment, a few new clothes, and a new lap top. Double sigh. It was, in essence, the last in a long line of steps that would get me where I needed to be.

The check wasn't there.

I kept my cool, walked back to my flat, then sat on the sofa and stared at my computer screen. To continue keeping my cool, I started playing a computer game; twice the game quit on me. It was as if the Almighty was saying, "No, THIS you need to deal with."

I imploded.

Between the staff meetings at work, the personal family challenges, my school work not getting done, and now the money not being there ... I lost it. I sat there and cried like a baby. My mind was racing. "I thought we were a team!" I mentally yelled at G-d. "I thought we had a deal: I do my part and you do yours!! I don't see this as you doing your part!!" It didn't stop there. "You took away my heart's desire, and replaced it with nothing!! Then you make me wait until the last minute on everything!! Can't we just once—just once—pay something ahead of time!?!"

Faith and Re-evaluation

I was past the point of frustration and disappointment. I was enraged!! And I was very, very careful. I had decided to live my life so as not to have to apologize for my words or my deeds; getting angry did not supersede that credo.

So what I didn't do became very important. The past practices of my life came to the forefront, but I didn't throw something, didn't use foul language or take my rage out on anyone else; I didn't pace the floor, bang my head against the wall, and I certainly didn't yell at my cat.

What I did do, however, was sit and cry; I talked to the Almighty; I told him that if the money was an issue He wanted to take control of, fine, take it, be good with it, and I wouldn't worry about it anymore. If all the things I couldn't control were things He wanted to be responsible for, FINE—have them! He could have my children, my soon-to-be-ex-husband, and all the other people in the world that I had no control over. He could have my job, my writing, my schooling, and all the things I couldn't do, couldn't control, or couldn't make a difference in. If the best thing I could do was NOTHING, then NOTHING was what I would do. However, if the best thing I could do was SOMETHING, then something would be what I would do as well.

He was very good with this.

As a defiant child, I vowed that I would show Him!! This was not going to break me!! I would continue to step up to the plate, continue to do my best, and certainly make good on my commitments. I would not sit and pout and whine incessantly about not getting my own way. I'd quit fighting Him to do things MY way; I would just surrender. I got up, got dressed, and went to Temple because I was bound to myself and to Him to do the right thing.

I had, through anger, learned what He couldn't teach me through pain; that He is the Almighty, that things will be done how He wants them done and when He wants them done, and there isn't anything I can do about it.

This is not an excuse, however, to shirk my duties. I had given up the struggle between what I wanted and what He wanted. Yes, I could tell Him what I wanted, what my heart's desire was/is, and where I think I need to be, but ultimately, it's still His decision.

It had been a very trying week; I had turned to my Rabbi on Monday for comfort and advice. I told her I thought I was losing my mind; she didn't comment. But she did tell me she thought I had

September

gotten to the top of the spiritual ladder, one in which the struggle was to give up the struggle: to be at the point where you lived totally trusting that G-d will work it out when you can't or shouldn't. My job, if you will, at this point was to listen, follow directions, and to be confident that all really was working out as G-d had planned.

Those were some mighty big leaps of faith for me; huge steps in the trust building arena.

So it was when I got up this morning, my plans lay along the line of going to Torah study and then going to pick up a carton of cigarettes for the week. I had decided to let G-d worry about the money aspect of it. I would listen and follow the guidance I received.

The guidance for today was to go to Torah study, treat myself to a coffee and pumpkin loaf at the coffee shop while putting ten dollars on my gift card for later, get the cigarettes at the grocer, and while I was there check to see if they had my antihistamine as my allergies are going to kick up. Well, sure enough, where they had been out of the brand I use over the summer, they had plenty in stock today and ON SALE, so I bought four boxes to get me mostly through the season.

While I was at it, the guidance said to check out the hamburger, canned veggies, and macaroni for my goulash; which showed all were either reasonable or on sale and quickly put in my cart. So, what are the odds, I asked, that the special treat of using chicken broth would be available so I could pick up a couple of cans?? They were – ten cans for $6!! A true bargain as they are normally $1.50 per can! Then the potato chips were there ... as was a nice bottle of red wine ... and in total $62.15 worth of groceries (that I had NOT planned on buying!) PLUS the cigarettes. I got change for a $20 and played the scratcher tickets. I won $20 on one ticket!!

Thinking that was as many blessings as I could stand for one day, I got the guidance that perhaps I should fill the gas tank at the low, low price of $2.56/gallon. To my surprise $25 filled the tank.

I talked to some good people along the way, giving a smile and chiding to help make their day a bit better. When I got home, I put everything away, invited some girlfriends over for dinner (that I just bought!!), put away the clean dishes, put a box of books in the closet, put some blankets away, and am about to take some big boxes for charity down to the car after I sand and polyurethane the

Faith and Re-evaluation

top of my desk and get it ready for the glass top that is to be delivered this week.

I didn't plan on spending $150 plus when I woke up; I didn't even know I HAD it to spend and am grateful that I did listen and do what was suggested as it increased my quality of life in the process. I'm realizing that planning my day is a great way to make sure I do my part, but I have to leave room so the Almighty can have some time too. I need to remember that when I listen, things turn out so very much better than I could ever plan.

I haven't checked the mail yet today, and win, lose, or draw, if the check is there, it's time; if it isn't, then it isn't time yet. Either way there is nothing I can do about it.

I'm very good with this.

September

SUMMARY

As you focused on GRACE this month, did you see a parallel to an issue in your own life? The following ten questions may help you gain new perspective on how to manage it.

Questions to ponder:

1. Is this issue bigger than me?

2. What is my part in resolving the issue?

3. Is now the right time?

4. What's stopping me?

5. How do I remove the barriers?

6. What resources will I need to get started?

7. What resources do I have?

Faith and Re-evaluation
Answers to Act on:

8. What isn't working?

9. What is working?

10. What's the next step?

To do List:

CLOSING NOTES

Well, here we are; you and I; just like we were a year ago. But, something has changed, we've changed; the issues we were dealing with a year ago have changed. Some have gotten better; some have gone away; and some are new to this year.

We are better than we were then; we have some new tools for handling the issues in our life; some different perspectives on how we view our life. This is good. There will be more challenges, more issues, more problems, but it is my hope that you have what you need to deal with them with courage, and understanding, and … with grace.

Life is a series of lessons; a series of opportunities to grow into the person the Almighty has chosen us to be. It's not always easy, it's not even always good; there's some ups and downs; beginnings and endings; calm and adventure.

It is my hope that being near brutally honest with you, that you've gained what you need to be honest with yourself, your family, your friends, and others you care about. It is my prayer that this work has helped you get to the next step in your journey. I'd like to know if it has.

Feel free to contact me at: cris_robins@hotmail.com with your comments, feedback, or questions.

I look forward to hearing from you.

With grace,
Ms. Christopher J. Robins

www.ingramcontent.com/pod-product-compliance
Lightning Source LLC
LaVergne TN
LVHW020928090426
835512LV00020B/3258